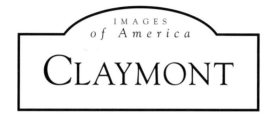

IMAGES
of America

CLAYMONT

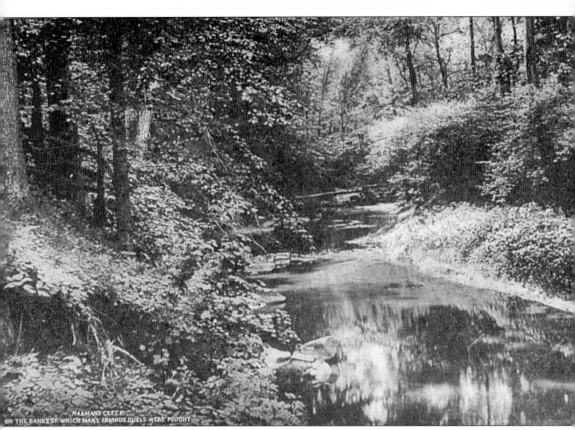

NAAMANS CREEK
ON THE BANKS OF WHICH MANY FAMOUS DUELS WERE FOUGHT

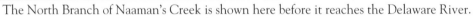

The North Branch of Naaman's Creek is shown here before it reaches the Delaware River.

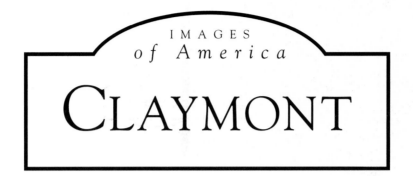

IMAGES
of America

CLAYMONT

Martha Schiek and Ray Hester

ARCADIA

Published by Arcadia Publishing,
an imprint of Tempus Publishing, Inc.
2 Cumberland Street
Charleston, SC 29401

Printed in Great Britain.

Library of Congress Catalog Card Number: 00-106602

For all general information contact Arcadia Publishing at:
Telephone 843-853-2070
Fax 843-853-0044
E-Mail sales@arcadiapublishing.com

For customer service and orders:
Toll-Free 1-888-313-2665
Visit us on the internet at http://www.arcadiapublishing.com

*This book was compiled from the life-long collections of Elizabeth Schiek
and discussions with Claymont residents of the past and present.
Mrs. Schiek collected Claymont photographs, newspaper articles, and written notes
for over 40 years, carefully documenting sources and details.
Her information was gathered from those who had lived this history
and/or had heard accounts from parents, grandparents, and others.*

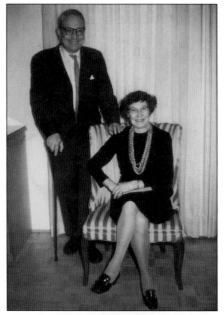

Dr. Allen and Elizabeth Schiek

CONTENTS

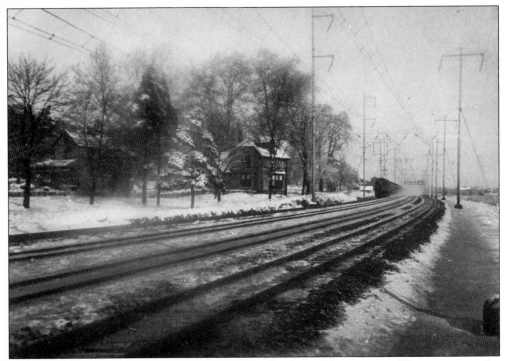

Looking north from Claymont Station, Raskob's (Archmere's) support staff houses are on the left, while the Delaware River is on the right. (Courtesy of Ruth Govatos Stein.)

ACKNOWLEDGMENTS

Without the meticulous notes and photographic collection of Elizabeth Schiek, this book would not have been possible. The support of the officers of the Claymont Historical Society was a great help. Fernando Franca (vice president), Theresa Fennick (secretary), Carolyn Mercadante (treasurer), and Judith Hester (research/historian) all were enthusiastic supporters and helpers. Special thanks goes to George E. Jackson, Steve Neff, and Grover (Jug) Elliott.

—Martha Schiek and Ray Hester

INTRODUCTION

The community now known as Claymont started on the banks of the Naaman's Creek where it empties into the Delaware River. This once rich ecosystem has been occupied steadily since before 1200 A.D. and has undergone numerous cultural and economic changes, most of which are still evident in the architecture and living patterns.

The first residents were aboriginal Indians of the Middle Woodland period (1100–1600 B.C.). Evidence of these early dwellers has been found along both sides of Naaman's Creek from its mouth on the Delaware to its sources on both branches.

The Dutch, who were the first Europeans to arrive, named the creek and the settlement Naamans, after the chief of the Lenape Indians residing along the creek. This little settlement grew rapidly and continuously from the 17th century through the 20th century, first with gristmills, farms, and related ancillary industries, and later with lumber mills, a steel mill, a chemical plant, and an ice cream plant.

As the nation grew, so grew Naamans from a little village into a small town, mirroring our country's development from the 1600s to the 1960s. The town sits strategically along the Delaware River, The Kings Highway, and the railroad. Claymont has been a two-way funnel for travel to and from Philadelphia and Washington, D.C., since colonial days. Philadelphia, the cradle of democracy, is 20 miles to the north and Washington, D.C., is 100 miles to the south. From the founding fathers to the molders of modern-day America, many have lived in Claymont and many more traversed its boundaries as America was carved out of the "new world."

Claymont's geographical position has been its strongest asset since its founding. The town's location forced it to see and experience America's development. Yet even today, after the dawning of a new millennium, Claymont somehow remains a small, proud, unincorporated "town," letting most of the hustle go by on the two interstate highways that literally cut the town into three slices.

Claymont became Claymont in 1856 after Reverend Clemson, the pastor of the Episcopal church, and his wife settled here. Mrs. Clemson had come from the family plantation, Claymont Court, in Charles Town, WV, and was a descendant of Bushrod Washington, greatnephew of George Washington. It was Mrs. Clemson who got the name changed in remembrance of her family home.

Claymont has been home and host to an impressive list of notable people. Among the earliest of these was a Swedish artist, Adolph-Ulrich Wertmüller, who had been appointed artist to the King of Sweden. His house still stands in the yard of the CitiSteel, USA Company. George Washington, "Mad" Anthony Wayne, and "Lighthorse" Harry Lee were frequent visitors of the Robinson House, one of several inns and taverns in Claymont along The King's Highway.

In 1859, renowned artist F.O.C. Darley, America's first illustrator of note, moved to Claymont. It was here that Darley finished the last two-thirds of his career and entertained Charles Dickens while he was on his 1867 American tour. It is also probable that he received Edgar Allen Poe, as well as some of the other authors for whom he illustrated, such as Longfellow, Irving, and Cooper.

In the late 1800s and early 1900s, Claymont attracted influential businessmen, such as J.J. Raskob and John Addicks, to settle permanently. The town became a summer residence for many Philadelphia businessmen. Raskob was the primary financier of the Empire State Building and founder of General Motors. From his Claymont residence, he and Joseph Kennedy Sr. planned Al Smith's presidential nomination and campaign.

Author Anne Parish was born in Claymont and wrote her 1925 Harper's Prize winning novel *The Perennial Bachelor* here. Her 1928 novel *All Kneeling* was made into the movie *Born to be Bad* starring Joan Fontaine.

Join us as we show you some of Claymont's 18th-century inns and farmhouses, 19th-century mansions, 20th-century industrial housing, and an Italianate palace. Discover the building that was hit with cannon balls from the British ship *Leopard* in 1812.

We will show you Claymont's fishing clubs, a lightkeeper's house, speak-easies, and the location of the last "legal" gun duel in the United States. Share some of the "Americanism" and patriotism of Claymont, its war memorials, and the seaplane training facility of World War I. Learn of the businesses along "the Pike" in Claymont Center. Visit the A&P meat counter and general store, Richardson Variety Store, and The American Store. Stop by the Claymont Trust Company, Buffington's News, and the cleaners. Have a soda at The Pantry. See the Claymont Fire Company's 1928 ambulance, Claymont's early churches, a camp meeting, and Church of the Ascension before it was moved across the Pike. Claymont's churches have always been, and continue to be, a vital thread in the community. Enjoy Claymont High School's sports teams, graduating classes, dances, and May Queen court. See where the students "hung out" and glance over the Worthland ball team. Learn about Claymont's 1923 Community Civic League, the Youth Council and its events, and Worthland and Overlook Colony's Community Centers. Being an unincorporated "town," Claymont has always had civic organizations to see that community needs were being met.

Yes, this is America, as it was from the 1630s through the 1950s. Take a little time, reminisce, and return again and again to find something new in each photograph. Even if you never lived in Claymont, you will experience *your* small-town America by viewing ours, and we proudly share it with you.

—Martha Schiek and Ray Hester
July 15, 2000

*All photos are courtesy of *The Elizabeth and Allen Schiek Claymont Collection* unless otherwise noted.

One

WHEN CLAYMONT
WAS NAAMANS

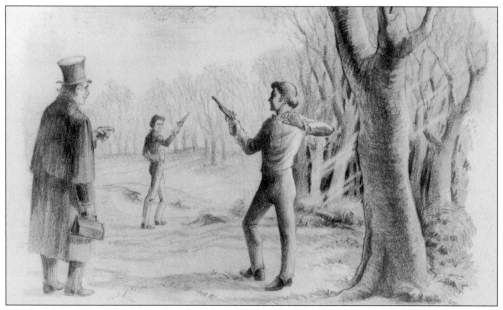

The hill located at Naaman's Road and Hickman Road was the site of the dueling grounds of the early 1800s. It is reported that men came from Pennsylvania to duel here after it was outlawed there. It is also reported that the last "legal" duel in America occurred here in 1830. That duel was between William Miller, a brilliant young Philadelphia attorney, and midshipman Charles G. Hunter of the U.S. Navy. Miller was mortally wounded and Hunter was discharged from the Navy by order of President Jackson, but he was later reinstated and served in the Mexican War. (Courtesy of Dawn Lamb.)

A Chronological History of Claymont

Compiled by Elizabeth Robelen Schiek in 1976

Claymont, one of the oldest inhabited territories in this part of the country, was originally called Naamans after Chief Naamans of the Delaware Nation.

1638	When Swedes arrive in Delaware, the community is occupied by the Lenape Indians.
1654	Tradition says Governor Riseing built a gristmill on Naaman's creek banks; there is no mention of this in his diaries, however.
1665	The Dutch, under Peter Styvesant, take over the community.
1674	The English under the Duke of York take control of this section and make land grants.
1680	The King's Highway is laid out. It is currently known as the Wilmington-Philadelphia Pike, or U.S. Rt. 13.
1701	Jasper Yates builds a gristmill.
1723	Alexander Robinson builds a colonial mansion, now known as the Robinson House, at the junction of Naaman's Road and Philadelphia Pike. General "Mad" Anthony Wayne, George Washington, Lafayette, and "Lighthorse" Harry Lee all visit or stay in the house.
c. 1750	The Practical Farmer Inn is erected at Harvey Road and Philadelphia Pike. It is torn down in 1974.
1778	A settlement is developed at Grubb's Landing along the Delaware River on land granted by William Penn to John Grubb.
1783	A.A. Grubb's house is built on The Kings Highway (became the Worth House & Holy Rosary convent).
1802	Adolph-Ulrich Wertmüller, artist to the King of Sweden, moves to Naamans to what is now CitiSteel property. He dies there in 1811. The house still stands.
1805	The Old Stone School building is erected at the corner of Darley Road and Philadelphia Pike.
1812	The first post office is established in Naamans.
1812–14	Several houses are bombarded from the Delaware River by the British. The Practical Farmer is hit.
1830	The last legal gun duel in the United States takes place. Near the Robinson House was a dueling ground, located here to escape authorities as dueling was outlawed in Pennsylvania.
1835	Churchman builds a sawmill along Naaman's Creek east of the Pike.

1837–38	The Philadelphia/Baltimore/Washington Railroad line is constructed along the river.
1845–50	Doctor J.T.M. Cardeza, the area's first doctor, is noted as being in Naamans.
1850–52	Reverend Clemson's wife, a descendent of George Washington, changes the name of the area from Naamans to Claymont. Her ancestral home is located near Charles Town, WV, and is called Claymont Court. Reverend Clemson was first rector of the Ascension Episcopal Church. Claymont Court was the home of Bushrod Washington, George's grandnephew.
1853	The Claymont Post Office moves to the railroad station at Naamans.
1854	The Church of the Ascension is built at the corner of Church Lane and Philadelphia Pike and is consecrated by Bishop Lee.
1859	Prominent book illustrator Felix Octavius Carr Darley (1821–1888) moves to Claymont to the "Chimney's," located at what is now the corner of the Pike and Darley Roads.
1866	The Church of Atonement is erected on land given by Thomas Kimber.
1870	Episcopal Priest Clemson establishes a boy's school in the house opposite Worthland ("Cedar Slope").
1885–56	The Baltimore & Ohio Railroad is built on the west side of Claymont.
1888	The Comstock Brick Yard is built on Naaman's Creek. Vernon's Grove developed (1890–1898).
1898	The Chester Traction Line (Trolley) is built through Claymont.
1899	The Ammonia (Chemical) Plant is built on Naaman's Creek, but lasts only a year.
1900–33	Vernon's Ice Cream plant operates at Naaman's and Ridge Roads.
1905	The post office located in railroad station at the foot of Manor Avenue comes about and The Stone School is expanded.
1911–17	This period sees rapid industrial expansion in the northern area of Claymont. A quick increase in population creates a need for educational facilities. Portable school buildings and church buildings are used. Different industries build small villages and schools to take care of their families. The villages of Worthland, National Aniline, and Overlook Colony are developed during this time. A strong spirit of "community" develops during this period and through the 1920s. Claymont really becomes a community, versus being a few industries, riverfront mansions, and farms.
1912	The General Chemical Company Delaware Works' Plant is erected at the Delaware-Pennsylvania state line, east of the Pike.
1914	The National Aniline Chemical Company Plant at the Delaware-Pennsylvania state line comes about.
1915	The Delaware Industrial School for Girls is established on Darley Road.
1916	Worth Steel is built.
1916–18	A private aviation school is built along the river between Myrtle Avenue and Naaman's Creek.
1918	Philadelphia Pike is paved with brick.
1919	School commissioners petition the state board of education to become the Claymont Special School District.
1920	The first Catholic Mass is celebrated in the home of Mr. and Mrs. Joel D. Gilen, of Worthland.
1920	The Green Lantern Theater is built on the Pike at Myrtle Avenue.
1921	The post office moves to McClure's Drug Store (later Claymont Pharmacy) on the Pike.
1921	The Holy Rosary Catholic Parish is established. Services are held in the building at Seminole Avenue and the Pike.
1921–22	A two-room brick building is constructed for black children, grades 1 to 6, at the Delaware-Pennsylvania state line. Grades 7 through 12 attend Howard in Wilmington.
1922	The Church of the Ascension moves across the Pike to its present location.
1923	The Claymont Trust Company opens at the Pike and Manor Avenue.
1924–25	The Green Street School building is constructed for grades 1 to 12.

1928	The Atonement Methodist Church Sunday School building is erected.
1928	The Claymont Volunteer Fire Company is organized.
1930	The post office moves into the original Claymont Trust Company building, next to the drug store.
1931	Claymont High School receives accreditation.
1931	Public kindergarten is organized in the Old Stone School, one of the first in the state.
1932	The Premonstratensian Fathers purchase Raskob's estate to use as a private boys school.
1936	Claymont gets its first dentist, Dr. Allen Schiek.
1936	The first permanent building for Holy Rosary Parish, the Rectory, is built.
1943	The Baker & Adamson Division of the General Chemical Company re-open buildings formerly closed by National Aniline company.
1943	The Delaware Industrial School for Girls becomes Woods Haven School.
1949	The Claymont Trust Company merges with the Wilmington Trust Company.
1950	Holy Rosary School is built. The school occupies 8 classrooms with the remaining space used for worship.
1952	The Court of Chancery orders the high school to desegregate.
1952	The Claymont Fire Company constructs a new building.
1953	The Green Street Elementary School opens with 25 classrooms; it costs $1 million to build.
1958–60	The present Holy Rosary Church is built, along with an addition to the school.
1959	The Atonement Church educational building is added.

(Post note: I-95 was opened in 1969; I-495 in 1972)

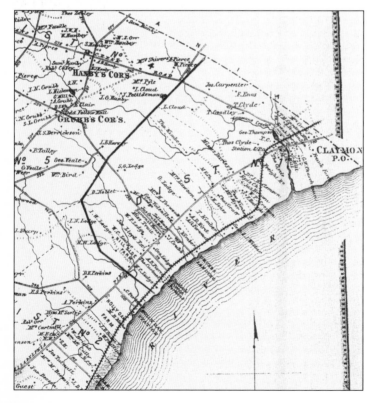

The *Beers Atlas* shows Brandywine Hundred and Claymont. Claymont is the upper right corner of the county and state, occupying about 4 square miles. The approximate boundaries of Naamans are highlighted on the map.

A headstone of the only known colonial cemetery in the vicinity of Naamans (Claymont). This 18th-century cemetery is on the state line on land now owned by Lawncroft Cemetery. The readable portion of this stone is, "T.W. died y 21 aged E R 1726." In 1937 there were over 24 stones observed by a WPA project. Two stones were moved to the Delaware County Historical Society. Two early families of Naamans, Rawson and Ford, were buried here. The cemetery has been vandalized and desecrated and today nothing remains.

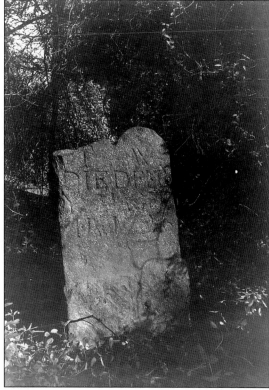

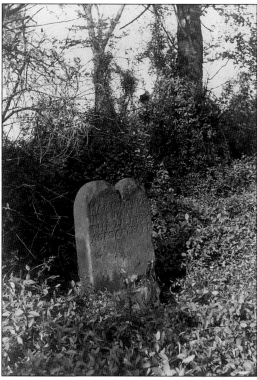

Another head stone, same period and location as above. It reads, "Mary Withys Died April the 21 1735, aged 64 years."

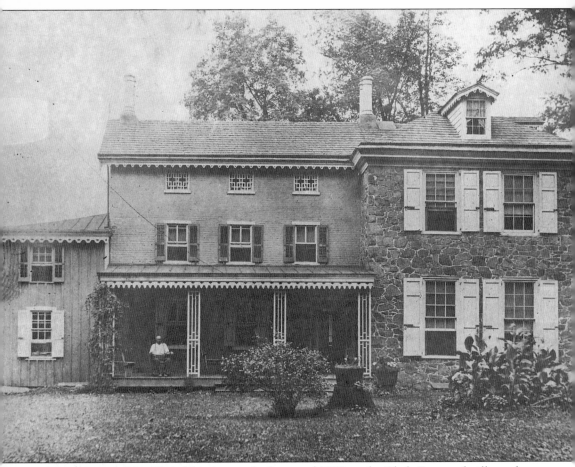

The first part of the Clyde Mansion was built around 1800 on the Clyde Farm and still stands on CitiSteel property (previously Worth Steel) on the east side of the Pike. In 1803, it was bought by Adolph-Ulrich Wertmüller from John Warder. Wertmüller had immigrated to America from Sweden in 1785 where he had been the King's artist. In 1794, he painted George Washington, a portrait that hangs in the National Art Gallery in Washington today. On January 8, 1801, Wertmüller married Elizabeth Henderson, granddaughter of Gustovus Hesslius, who was an artist and brother of Andreas Hesslius. Andreas was pastor of Old Swedes Church in Philadelphia from 1712 to 1713. Wertmüller died at his Naamans' home on October 5, 1811, and is buried at Old Swedes Church in Philadelphia.

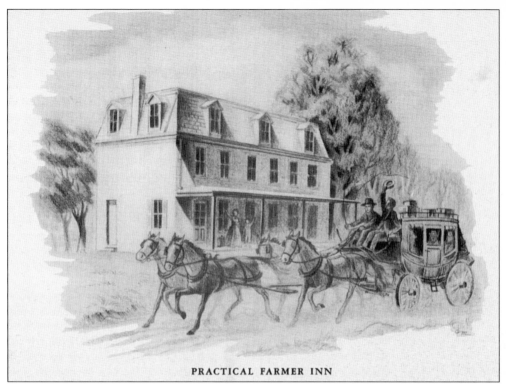

PRACTICAL FARMER INN

This is an artist's rendering of the Practical Farmer Inn (see p. 28 for details). (Courtesy of Dawn Lamb.)

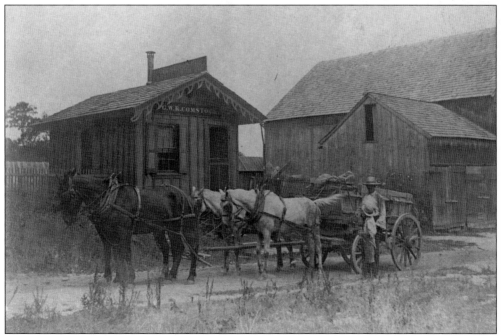

Nineteenth-century industry on Naaman's Creek included the Comstock Brick Yard. The loading docks on Naaman's Creek had two platforms, one for low and high tide.

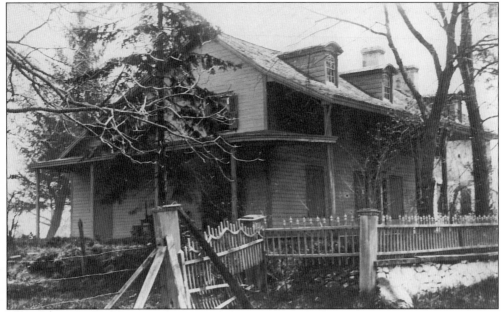

The Robinson House at Philadelphia Pike and Naaman's Road is pictured here around 1905, prior to renovations. Built as a three-room dwelling around 1723, the home has undergone several renovations. It is believed that the blockhouse may have been built on the property by Johan Rising in the 1650s. The name comes from Col. Thomas Robinson, who acquired the property around 1738.

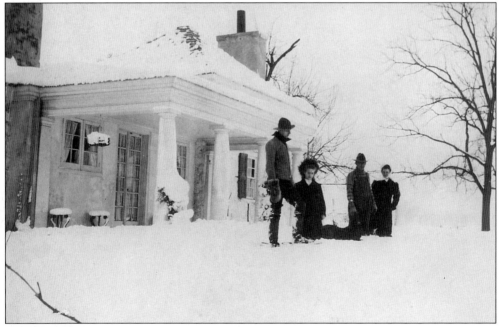

This pre-1912 photo of the Robinson House shows it at a time when it was used by artists as a studio and a residence. Most of them were students of Howard Pyle, who primarily taught in his Wilmington studio. Pyle taught N.C. Wyeth and many other well-known artists. Among those pictured are Henry J. Peels, T.V. Ivory, Herbert Moore, Rosco E. Schroder, and Gayle Hoskins.

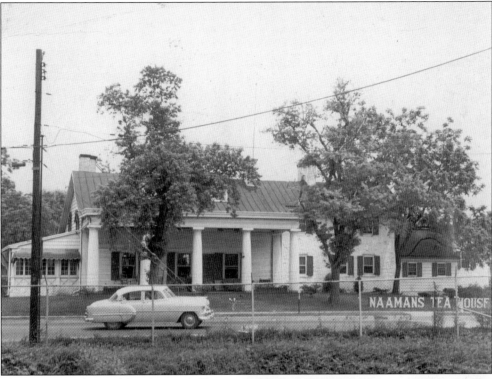

This is a 1953 photo of the Naaman's Tea House (the Robinson House), a popular restaurant for several years. Charles W. Robinson acquired the house in the early 1900s. He was unrelated to the original owner, Colonel Robinson. The state of Delaware acquired the property in 1967. The Friends of the Robinson House now give tours of the house.

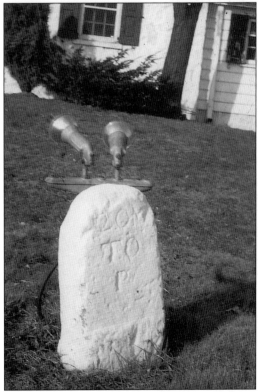

A mile marker at the corner of Naaman's Road and The Kings Highway (now Philadelphia Pike) is shown here. It notes that Philadelphia is 20 miles away, "20 M to P."

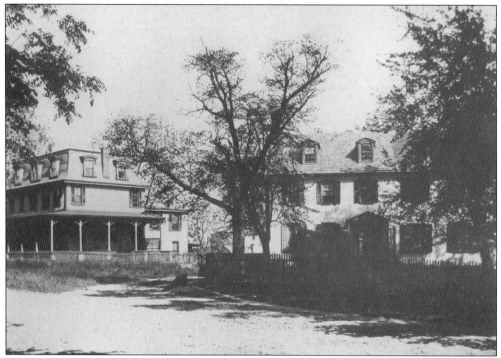

These two houses stood on the east side of Philadelphia Pike (in the foreground), on the north side of Naaman's Creek. They were originally built around 1790, and were torn down in 1901 for the rerouting of the railroad. The left house belonged to the Danzenbaker family and the house on the right belonged to the Grahams and Habbarts.

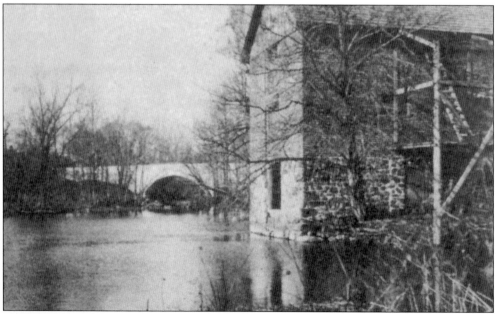

The King's Highway was laid out in 1680, linking Wilmington and Philadelphia. In 1802, this stone toll bridge was installed over Naaman's Creek near the original forge. It was torn out in the 1960s to allow the construction of an interstate highway.

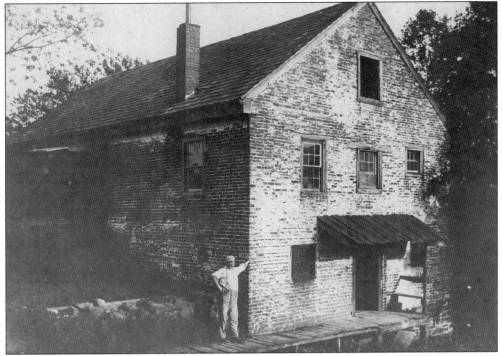

Naaman's Grist Mill was located on the north side of Naaman's Creek, east of The Kings Highway ("The Pike"). Built around 1701, it was originally a one-story stone building belonging to Jasper Yates. In 1749, Samuel Hendrickson added a second story of brick. It was owned by Charlie Price in 1901 when the Pennsylvania Rail Road bought it and tore it down to reroute the railroad. Price is in this pre-1901 picture. Large quantities of grain was converted into flour and shipped to Philadelphia and Wilmington markets.

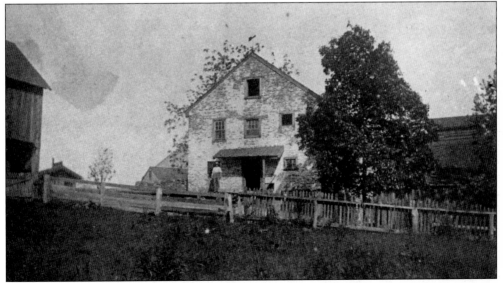

Shown here, from left to right, in this 1898 photo are the Graham barn, the top of the Comstock Brickyard office, the barn belonging to Danzenbaker House, the gristmill, and Churchman's sawmill.

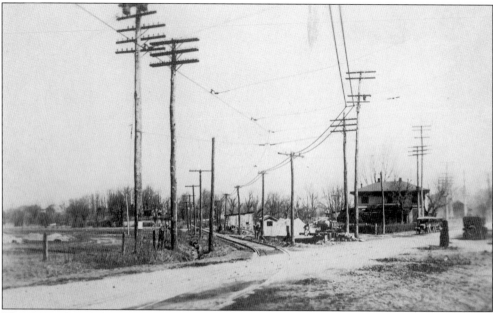

The original Naaman's Station is shown here around 1901 from Philadelphia Pike prior to Worth Steel.

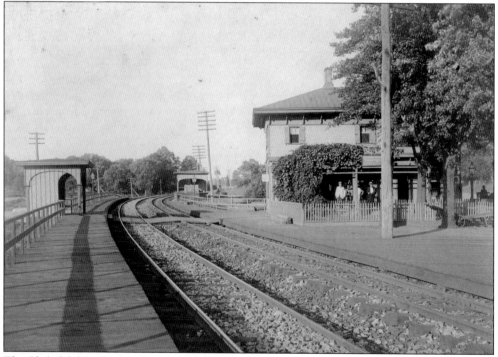

The Philadelphia, Wilmington, and Baltimore Railroad came to Naamans in 1838. Naaman's Station, pictured here in 1901, stood where CitiSteel's rail tracks cross Philadelphia Pike today. Pictured here, from left to right, are William Habbart, Eben Baldwin, and Enos Whitman. The Pennsylvania Railroad bought the line in 1901; the station was relocated to the foot of Myrtle Avenue, then in 1905 it moved to the bottom of Manor Avenue.

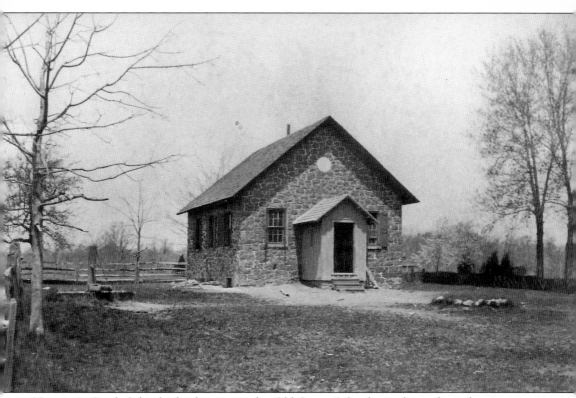

Naaman's Creek School, also known as the Old Stone School, was located at what is now Darley Road and Philadelphia Pike. The school was established in 1805 on ground deeded to a group of Brandywine Hundred citizens by John Dickinson in 1803. Dickinson was a signer of the United States Constitution. The school provided public education in this area for about 25 years before the Delaware legislature passed any effective laws for public education. The building was the headquarters of pubic education in Claymont until 1922 and was used for educational purposes into the 1950s. The first Episcopal church services were held here by Bishop Lee in 1843.

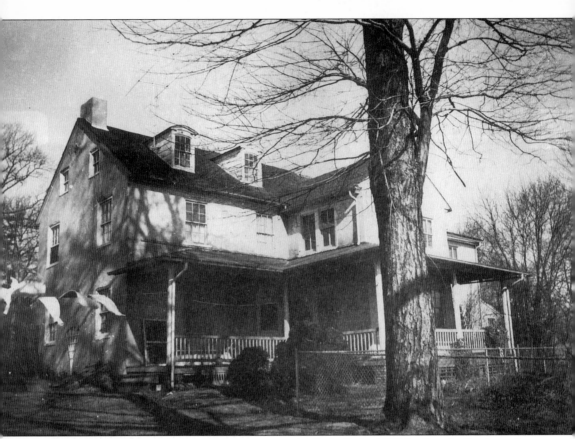

The Casey House on Manor Avenue was originally built in 1760 by Joseph Gordy and was expanded around 1848. Gordy's granddaughter married Robert Casey—thus, the Casey name in the lineage. Gordy-Casey descendants have lived in the house ever since. The current residents, Jim and Linda Rambo, are descendants. Jim's great-grandmother, Kathryn Casey, wrote extensive notes on the family. The original Rambo, Peter, arrived on the *Kalmar Nyckel*, a Swedish ship. The original farm adjoined the Kimber Farm (now Archmere) on the north and went south to what is now Wiltshire Road. From the Pike, the farm went east to the Pennsylvania Railroad. When the railroad route was changed, the railroad bought most of the farm and put in Manor Avenue for a station. The original entrance to the farm was between what is today a bank and sub shop.

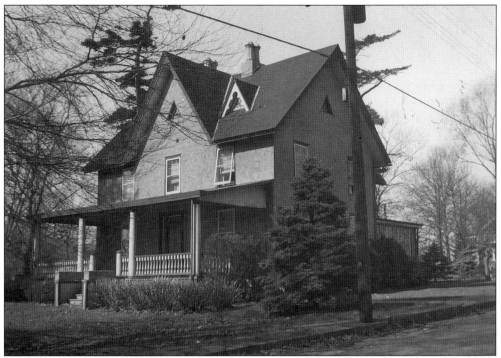

This house on Manor Avenue was originally part of the Casey Farm and is supposed to have been one of the barns. The photo was taken around 1952.

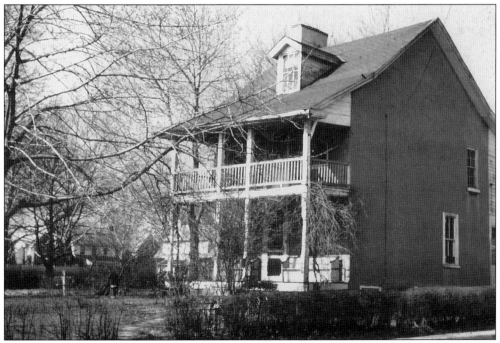

The Lawson Farmhouse was built in the late 1700s or early 1800s. Today the house would be located on Green Street and Lawson Avenue; the original farm, however, lay to the west and included the land where the schools are today.

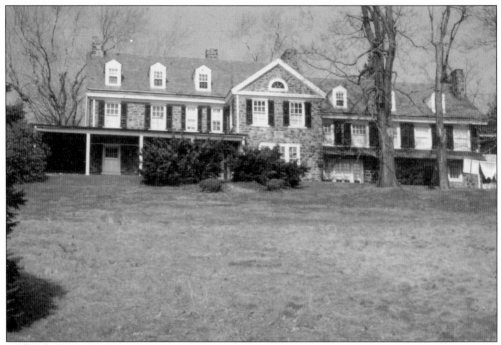

The right wing of the A.A. Grubb House was built in 1783. The left wing was added in 1919 by E.A. Worth after he established Worth Steel in Claymont. It was sold in 1953 to the Holy Rosary Church for use as a convent for the Sisters of St. Joseph.

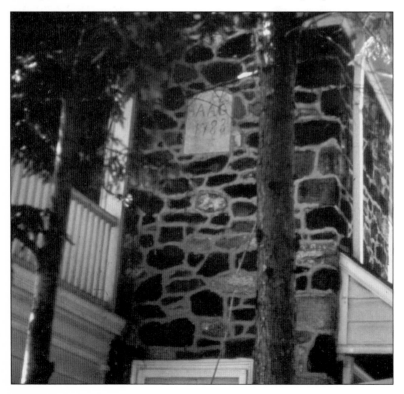

The date stone for the A.A. Grubb House is shown here.

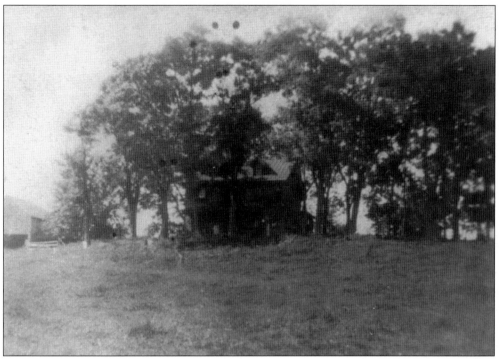

The A.A. Grubb House's date stone on the upper section of north wall shows "A.A. Grubb 1783." This photo was taken October 5, 1905, prior to the major alteration of the house.

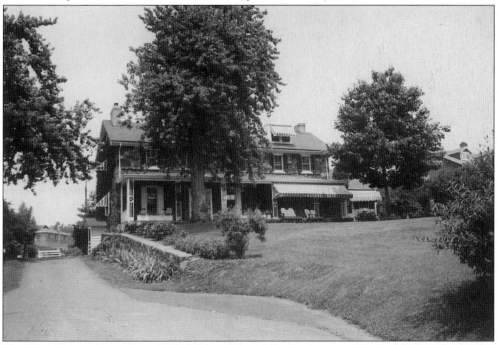

The Burr House, located on Philadelphia Pike, is shown here as it looked before the Burger King was built in front of it. The house was built in 1756 and had been owned by Lott Cloud in the mid-1800s.

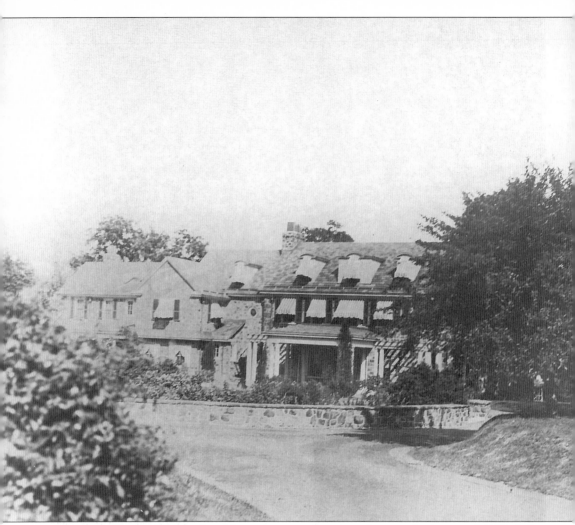

The original part of the Lackey Mansion, as it is known today, was built around 1738. It has undergone extensive renovations over the years, but it originally had a mansard roof. The original land grant was 600 acres to John Grubb, but at the time the house was built it had 56 acres on both sides of the Pike (The Kings Highway). In 1798, Frances Daumas, a French refugee from Santo Domingo, purchased the property. His wife ran the Practical Farmer. In 1805, the property was sold to the Willing family. Thomas Willing Francis was the grandfather of Thomas Francis Bayard, ambassador to Great Britain. Thomas Grubb, Esq., owned the adjoining estate, Stockdales, and in 1823 bought the Willing property.

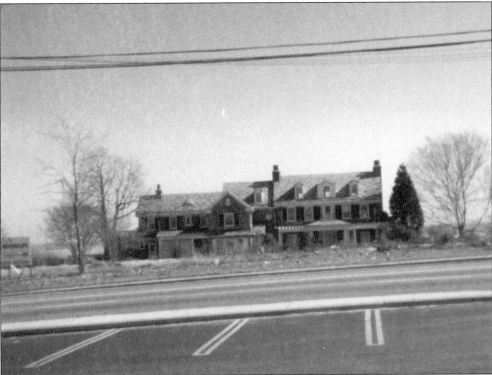

Frank D. Lackey bought this property in 1912. Lackey was in the banking and brokerage business. He significantly remodeled the house in 1917 at a cost of $180,000. In the 1970s, the land was parceled and sold. Housing was built in the rear and a store and McDonalds was constructed in the front. Today, the house serves as a residence and a computer software company. (History courtesy of Joseph and Faith Elad.)

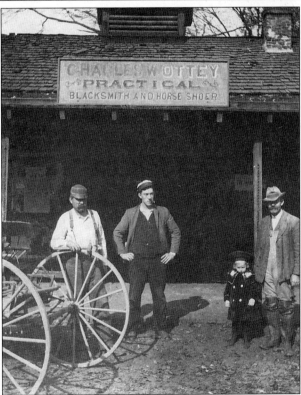

Charlie Ottey's Blacksmith Shop stood at the southwest corner of Naaman's Bridge on The Kings Highway (Philadelphia Pike). Pictured from left to right in this c. 1905 photograph are Charles Ottey, Herbert Hemphill, Paul Baldieru, and Mr. William Hoopes of Hoops Mills.

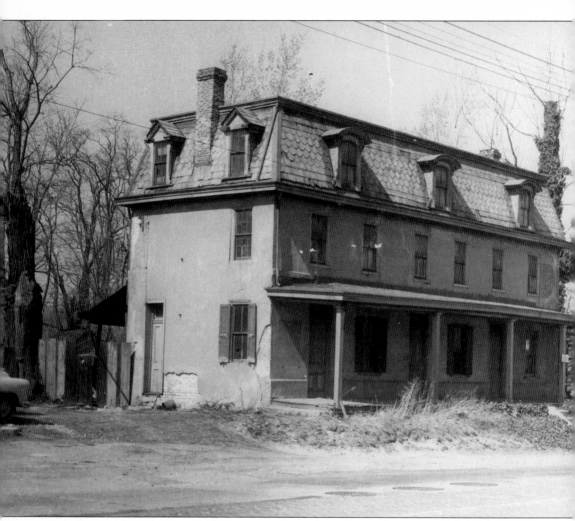

Built before 1750, the Practical Farmer was located on the north corner of Philadelphia Pike and Harvey Road. First known as the Queen of France Tavern, it became the "Guillotined Queen of France" and the sign showed the bloody trunk of a beheaded woman. Public opinion forced the sign to be removed and the name was changed to "The Woman Who Was Silent." Around 1796, the name changed to the Practical Farmer. In 1803, the inn belonged to Mrs. Travers, a refugee from Santo Domingo who lived in what was to become the Lackey Mansion. It was always a popular place for commerce and was a stopping place for stage coaches and horsemen due to its location midway between Wilmington and Chester on the Pike. There was also a turnpike tollgate next door. The older Swan Inn was on the south side of Harvey Road.

Two

THE VICTORIAN ERA: CLAYMONT BECOMES CLAYMONT

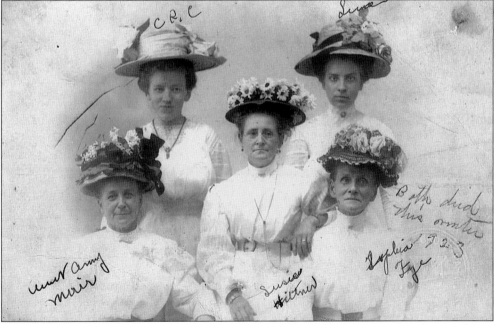

These Casey family relatives, from left to right, are as follows: (front) Aunt Amy (Aunt of Cora and Lena) and Sophia Fye; (middle) Susie Hittner; (back) Cora Casey and Lena Casey. (Courtesy of Linda K. Rambo.)

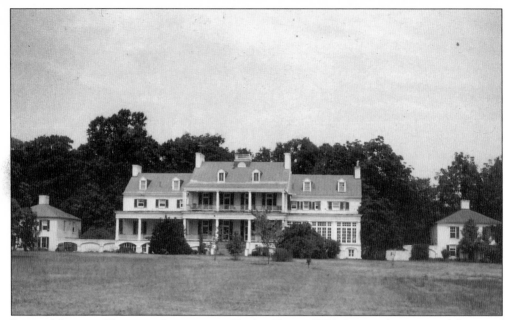

Pictured here is Claymont Court, near Charles Town, WV. It was the ancestral home of Reverend Clemson's wife, who was a descendent of Bushrod Washington, greatnephew of George Washington. Reverend Clemson was an Episcopal pastor who first had a church in Marcus Hook, PA. After becoming rector of the Church of the Ascension in Naamans, he moved here with his wife into the church's rectory. In 1854 she named the hill and area around the rectory Claymont, a name which quickly spread as the new name to the whole of what is now known as Claymont.

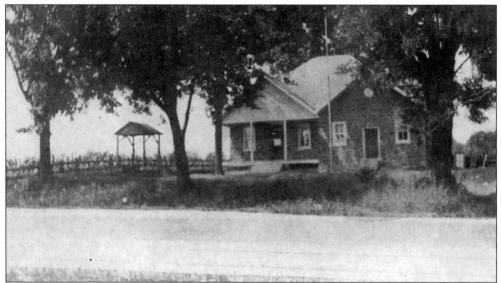

In 1905, Naaman's Creek School was expanded to twice its original size. A large interior arch between the new and old sections maintained the school as a one-room building. The Woman's Club of Claymont founded the Claymont Library in this building in the late 1920s. It was administrated by a four-member library commission from 1945 until July 1, 1975, when the New Castle County Department of Libraries assumed full responsibility.

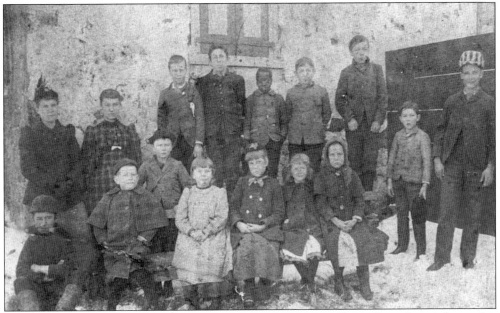

Pictured here is the Naaman's Creek School class of 1893–94. Shown here, from left to right, are the following: (front) Elwood McBride, Harry Cochran, Herman Polis, Tina Polis, Lillie Ottey (younger sister of the teacher), Eva Bigger, and Katie Shute; (back) Blanche Ottey (teacher), Alice Hoops, Jim Shute, Lewis Lloyd, Willie Wilson, Harry Forward, Willie Grubb, Herb Hemphill, and Jack Shute. This photo indicates that the school was integrated; however, other than the picture, there is no record of how many black children may have attended the school prior to the construction of the State Line School for African-American children.

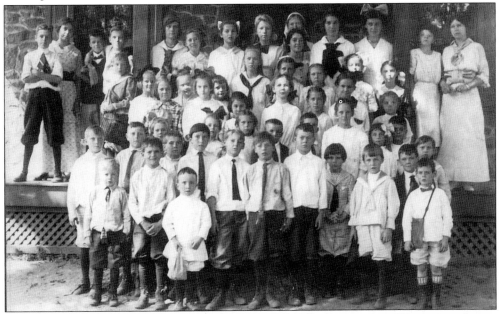

This is a *c.* 1915 Naaman's School (Old Stone School) class picture. (Given in memory of Alice Vernon Richardson and Elizabeth Vernon Hastings, of the "Vernon Ice Cream" plant family.)

Felix Octavius Carr Darley (1821–1888), America's first illustrator of note, moved to Claymont in 1859. Darley illustrated for a lot the famous writers of the day, including Edgar A. Poe, Fenimore Cooper, Nathaniel Hawthorne, Washington Irving, Henry Wadsworth Longfellow, Harriet Beecher Stowe, and others. He was known as Charles Dickens' American illustrator. Dickens visited Darley in 1868 for a few days rest on his tiring lecture tours between Philadelphia, Baltimore, and Washington, D.C.

Felix Darley had just married Ms. Jenny G. Colburn of Cambridge, MA, at the time that this picture was taken. They were preceded at the Claymont home, then called "The Chimneys" (for it's English chimney pots), by two of Felix's brothers and two of his sisters. The siblings had moved to the house in 1843 from the family home in Philadelphia. Felix changed the name of the home to "The Wren's Nest," in honor of Mrs. Darley, "his little Wren."

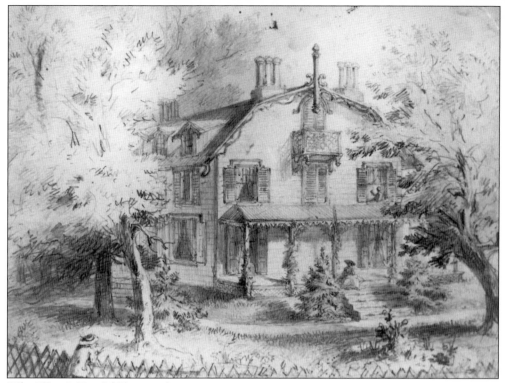

"The Wren's Nest" (Claymont) was drawn by Felix Darley shortly after he moved into it in 1859.

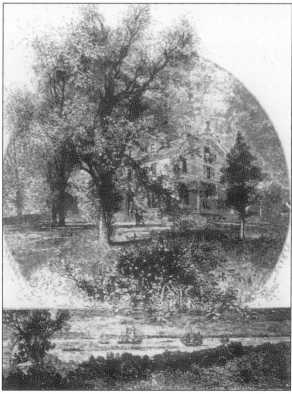

The Wren's Nest had a large yard and a river view in 1879. Tall ships could be seen going up and down on the Delaware River from the home's porch and front windows. Today, only a very small portion of the river can be seen due to intervening trees and buildings.

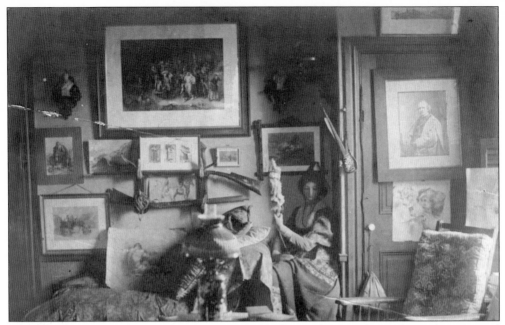

This picture shows Darley's studio where over half of his works were done. The studio is located in the Wren's Nest. Darley was the first American illustrator to move away from the key publishing centers of New York and Philadelphia to the "suburbs." The home in Claymont was only a brief walk from the major rail line, so he could take his work regularly to the publisher.

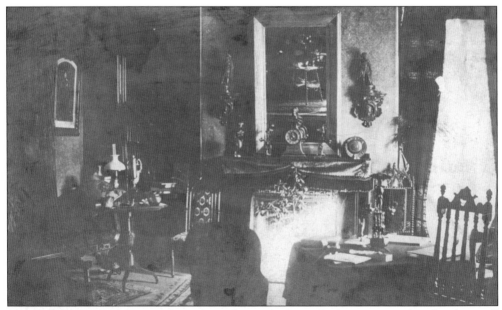

A view of the Darley's front parlor is shown here. The house had 17 rooms and 13 fireplaces, all needed by the 6 adults that lived together in the house for up to 58 years (from 1859 until Mrs. Darley's death in 1916).

The Reverend John B. Clemson, D.D., served the Church of the Ascension from 1852 until 1873. Reverend Clemson donated land on the corner of Church Lane on the east side of Philadelphia Pike (across the street from the present-day location) for the church in 1850.

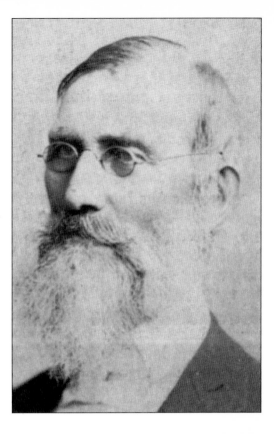

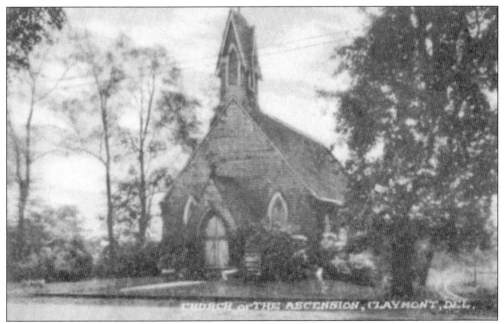

The Church of the Ascension when it was on the corner of Philadelphia Pike and Church Lane is shown here around 1915 (Church Lane is the rutted road to the right).

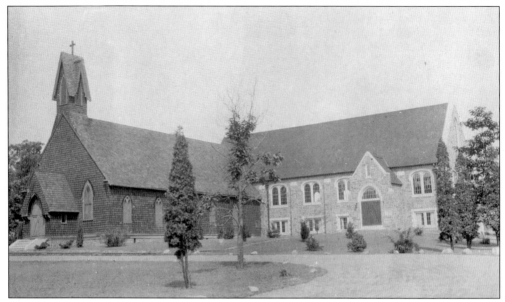

This photograph shows the Church of the Ascension after it was moved across the Philadelphia Pike in 1927 to its present location.

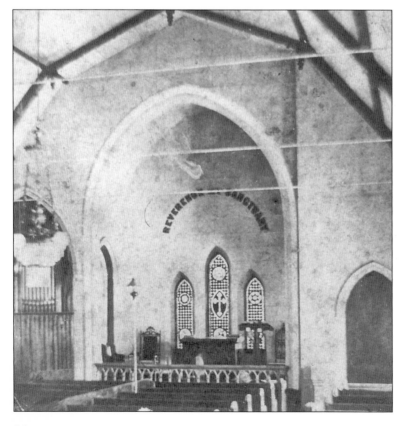

The Church of the Ascension's alter is shown here around 1860.

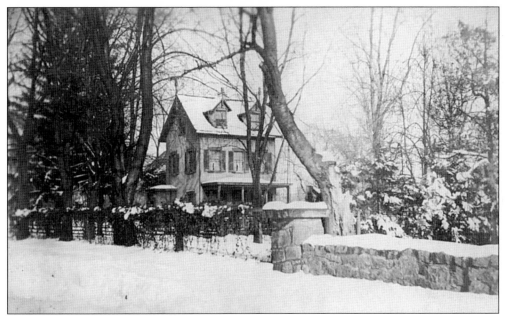

This home, located on Myrtle Avenue, was built before 1868 by the Church of the Ascension for a rectory prior to one being built near the new church. It was identified on the 1868 *Beers Atlas* and was demolished for the constructing of I-495.

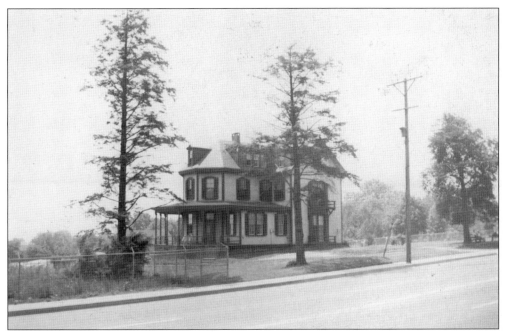

This house, known as Cedar Slope, was on the east side of the Pike where it intersects I-495 today. It was owned by the Episcopal Church in the 1850s, and Reverend Clemson ran a boy's school here.

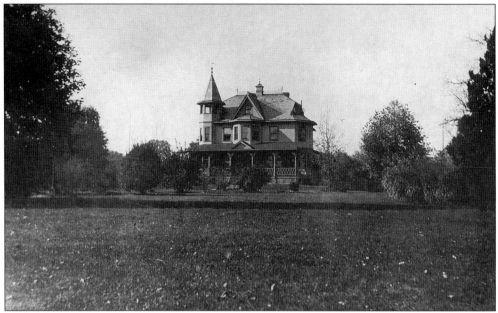

This residence was built in 1892 by Traver Dickerson, a Philadelphia shipbuilder. It was located on Philadelphia Pike's west side between the Church of the Ascension Rectory and Worthland (Knollwood) and was torn down for the building of I-495 in the 1970s.

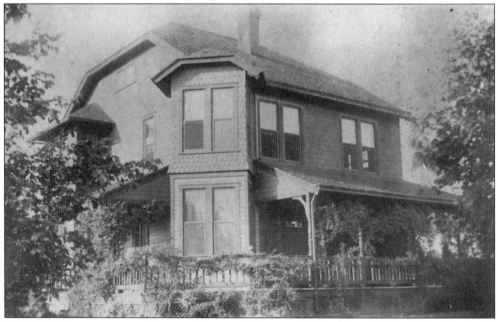

The Tage House, home of Anna, Clara, and Emma, was built in 1892 by Mrs. Darley. It was located north of the Church of the Ascension Rectory and was demolished to make way for I-495.

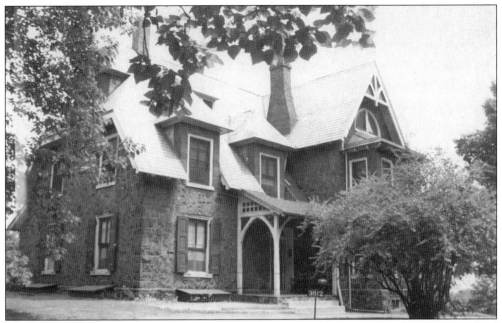

Built in the 1850s and originally part of the Clyde Farm, this house was used by the Church of the Ascension as a girl's school. Later, it became the summer home for Mrs. Jeans of Philadelphia. The original building had burned in 1875; this is the rebuilt home, which was demolished to allow the construction of I-495.

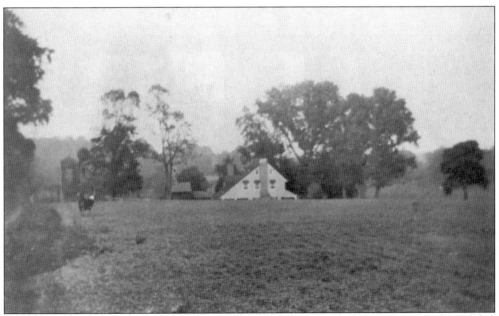

Prior to building Worth Steel (now CitiSteel), this farm was located on the west side of Philadelphia Pike. It was originally part of Clyde Farm. Clyde had given this piece of property to his son when he married Ms. Grubb. The house in the picture was built around 1901 by the Marion family to replace the original home, which was destroyed by fire and stood behind what is now Balfour Avenue in Knollwood (Worthland).

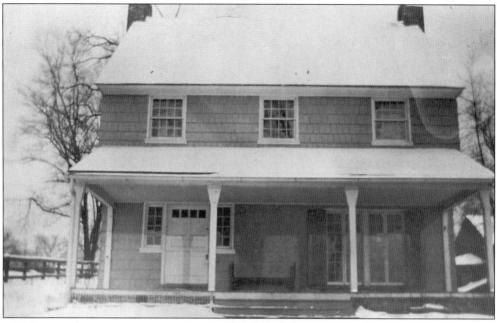

This is a view from the front of the Marion House.

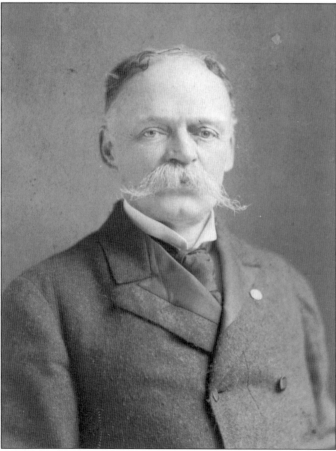

J. Edward O'Sullivan Addicks is shown here in a photo taken around 1904. Mr. Addicks made his fortune in natural gas and moved to Delaware where he thought that he could "purchase" a seat in the Senate. Unfortunately for him, he was unsuccessful. It is believed that his failed effort resulted in the passing of the 17th amendment to the Constitution (1913), making the election of senators determined by popular vote. Born in 1841, Addicks moved to Claymont in 1877.

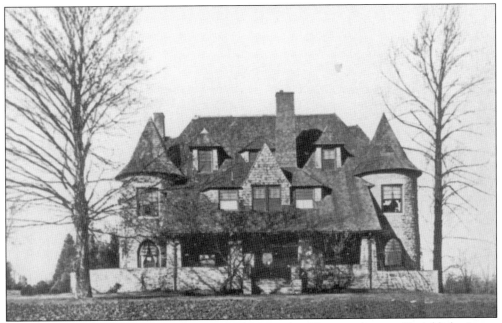

Miraflores, shown above in a riverfront view, became the Claymont home of J. Addicks. It was built by Mrs. Wilson, who later married J. Addicks. She named Myrtle Avenue for the ground cover along the street. Landscaping for the estate was done by John Cochran of Riverton, NJ. A view of the parlor appears below. (Both courtesy of Judge and Mrs. Elwood Melson.)

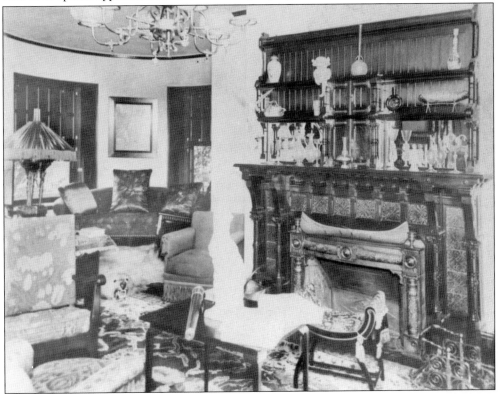

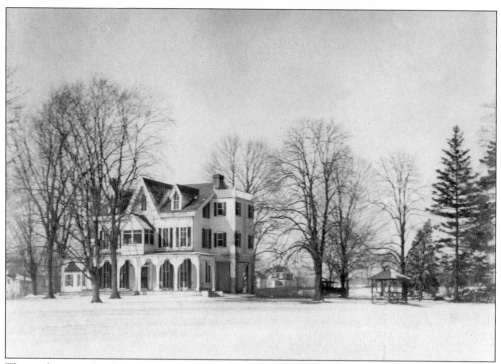

These photographs show a riverside view (above) and a front view (below) of the Troutman estate, Marshall Hill. Originally this was part of the Thomas Kimber farm. Marshall Hill was built by Mr. Troutman, a wealthy Philadelphia banker. He used most of the property to raise hay for his horses in Philadelphia, which he shipped by rail.

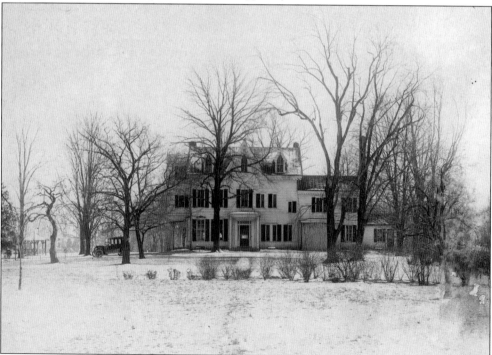

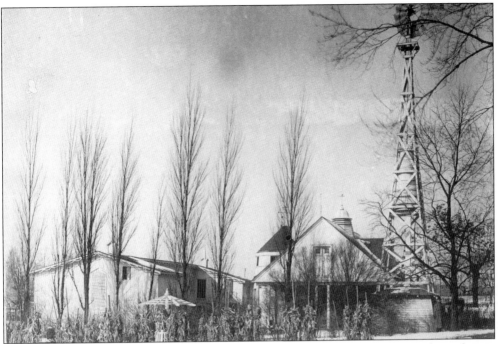

Pictured here is the Troutman estate in the late 1800s. From left to right are the icehouse, carriagehouse, and the windmill. The man standing by the windmill is D.C. Wharton Smith, son-in-law of Mr. Troutman. It was the job of William Danzenbaker and George Lloyd to store ice in the icehouse in winter and to fill the barn with hay in summer.

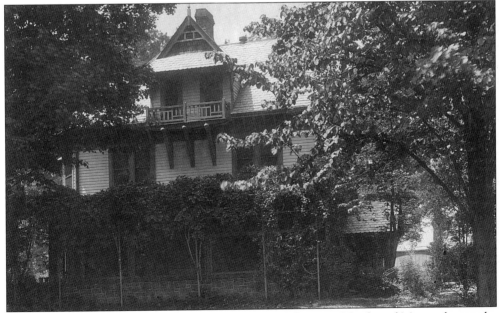

Woodsedge (see p. 45), located on a small lane that ran between Myrtle and Manor close to the railroad tracks, was first owned by Mrs. Ida Carr Wilson before she married John Edward O'Sullivan Addicks. It was then purchased by J.J. Raskob, who lived there from 1916 to 1917 while the present Archmere was being built. It burned in 1952.

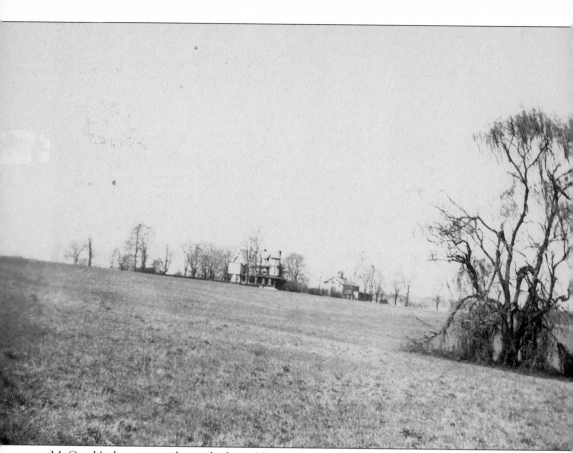

McComb's house was located along Naaman's Creek (South Branch) where Brookview Apartments are today. The McComb Farm originally ran from Philadelphia Pike back to the B&O Railroad, along Darley Road, and down to where the Atonement Methodist Church is located today. In the 1860s, it was part of a larger tract owned by Thomas Kimber. At that time, the farm ran from the CSX Railroad down to the Delaware River and from Darley Road to a property line just north of what is now Seminole Avenue (excluding the Naaman's Creek School). Thomas Kimber, in 1867, was president and co-founder of the "Delaware Association for the Mutual Improvement and Education of Colored People," which established schools for blacks throughout the state (Source courtesy of the 1892 *Historical and Biographical Dictionary of Delaware*).

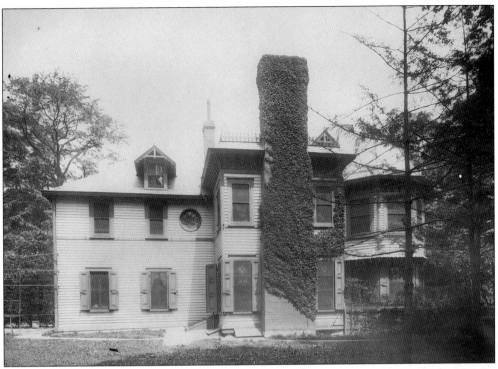

The west side of Woodsedge is shown here (also see p. 43).

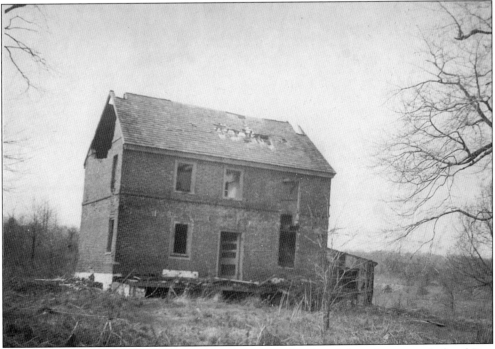

McComb's tenant house was built in two sections, one brick and the other stone. It faced Post Road (Philadelphia Pike) in this photograph from around 1954. The brick likely came from the Claymont Brick Yard.

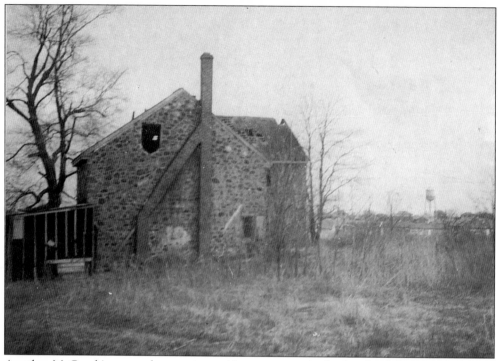

Another McComb's tenant house, pictured here, was on the back side of the farm, and faced the B&O Railroad, now the CRX, on the west border of Claymont, near the Ardens.

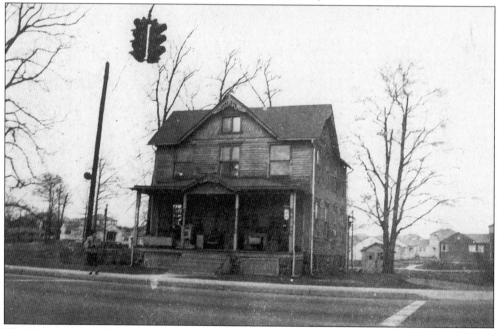

This house was on the entrance lane to McComb's house and was the home for his coachman, Mr. Whitman. It was located opposite the head of Manor Avenue on the west side of Philadelphia Pike and was later Sinclair's Antique Shop. The photograph was taken around 1952.

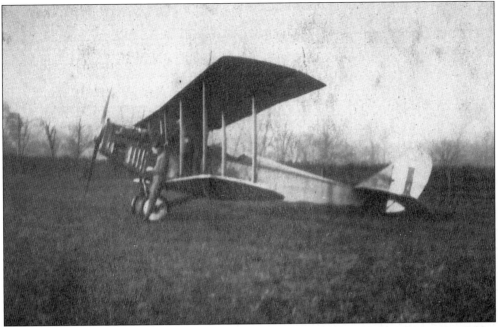

A bi-plane is shown here at McComb's "airpark" at Philadelphia Pike and Darley Road. The man is likely Jim Sinclair, who lived on the McComb Farm and flew his plane out of the field. He gave rides to the local people and reportedly sponsored air shows here in the 1940s. (Courtesy of Linda K. Rambo.)

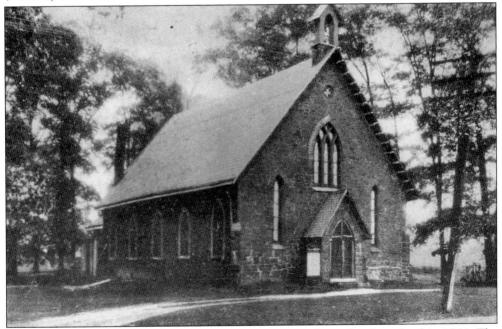

The Church of the Atonement, built in 1866, was started as a Sunday school in 1864. The meeting that determined this was held over Frank Ford's grocery store, located opposite the Robinson House. In 1866, Thomas Kimber, a Quaker, donated the land and $2,500 to build the church, with one condition—that there would be no cross put on it.

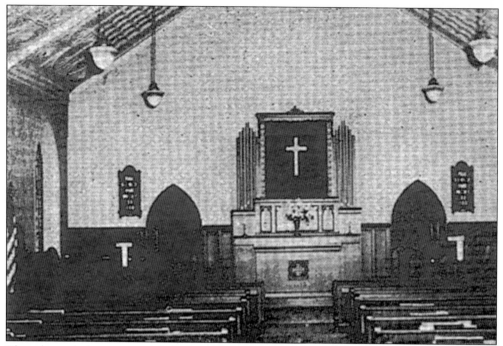

The alter of Atonement Methodist Church is shown here around 1946. (Courtesy of Atonement Church and Elizabeth Schiek.)

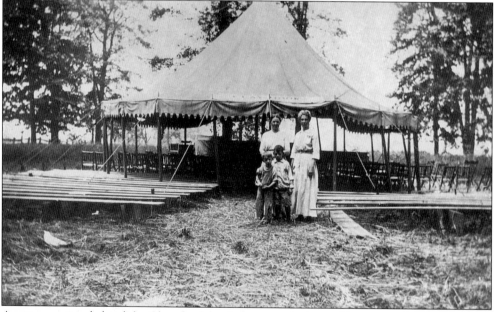

A camp meeting behind the Church of the Atonement is pictured here around 1918. The boys are, from left to right, Ennis Whiteman and Willard Whiteman. The ladies, from left to right, are Mrs. Anna Whiteman and Mrs. Emely Laird.

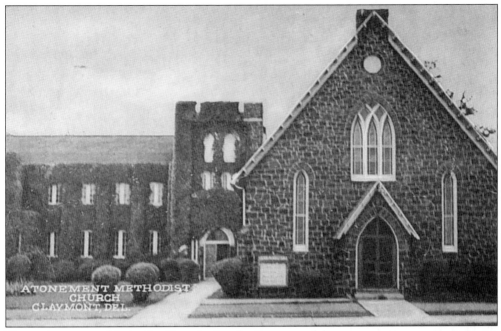

This is Atonement Methodist Church after the 1927 remodeling.

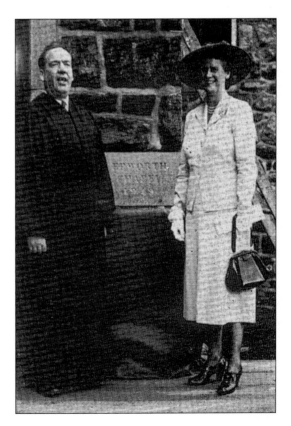

The Reverend and Mrs. Spence Jr. are pictured here. Reverend Spence was pastor when the 1945 addition was completed.

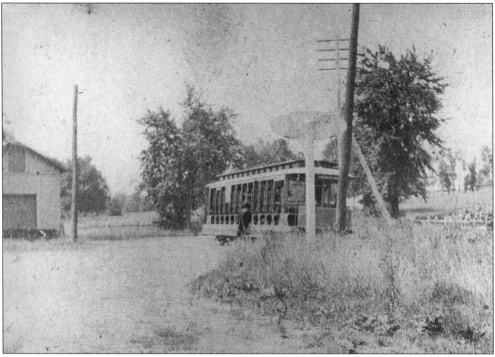

A Wilmington-Chester Trolley car from 1891 is shown where the line crossed Philadelphia Pike just south of Naaman's Creek.

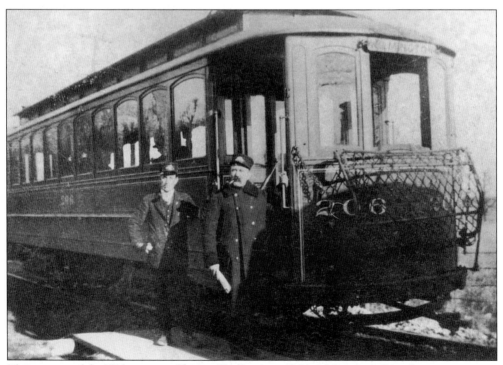

This picture of the Wilmington-Chester Trolley was taken at Naaman's Switch.

The original Stockdale Avenue
became known as Shell Road
when General Wistar used shells
to pave it. Tracks of the
Wilmington-Chester Trolley line
are visible on the right. It turned
right toward Wilmington where
Temple Avenue is now. This is
where the Governor Printz
Boulevard runs from Philadelphia
Pike toward the river today.

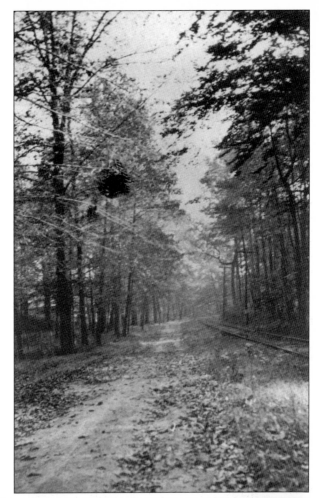

Rivercroft was the home of Frank
Graff in 1868. This was one of two
homes located along Shell Road
where the Claymont Garden
Apartments, located on the
northeast corner of Governor
Printz Boulevard and Philadelphia
Pike, are today. Mrs. Allan
Speakman later owned the house
and operated a rest home for the
elderly there.

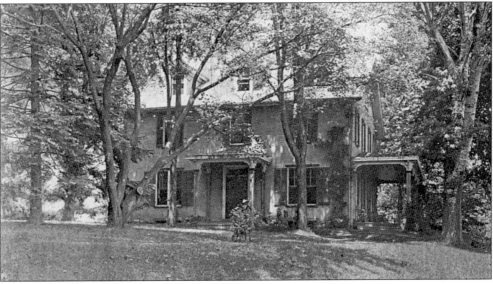

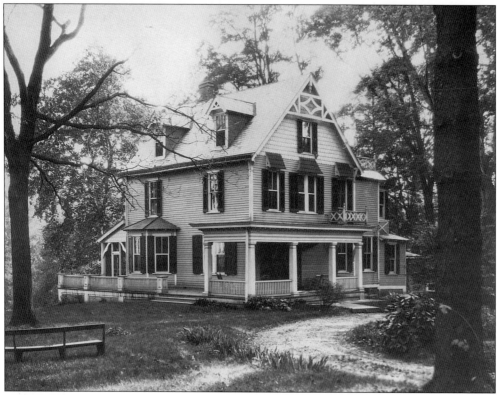

Built by Sloan around 1870, this home was later owned by the Cobbs, then the Evans, and eventually William Mullin. The house was also where the Claymont Garden Apartments are today. The photograph was taken around 1930.

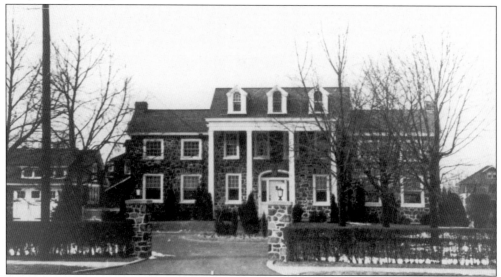

The Farrow Home, known recently as the "Coach House," was located on the Pike between Harvey Road and Maple Lane. The Farrows lived here in the 1940s. After they sold the home it became a lodge house and had other uses, before becoming a restaurant. (Courtesy of Daniel Farrow.)

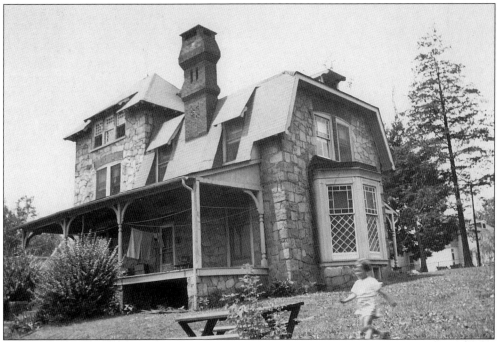

The home of William Cloud, son of Lott Cloud, is shown here around 1959. It is located on the east side of Philadelphia Pike near the present Eastpoint Apartments. William married Reverend Clemson's daughter, which left him financially well off and a "country gentleman."

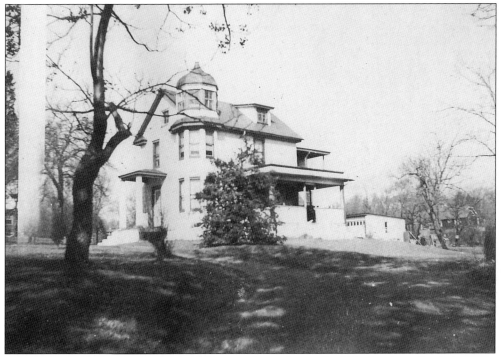

The John Bird House, built in 1909, was located on Grubb's Landing Road between Philadelphia Pike and Governor Printz Road.

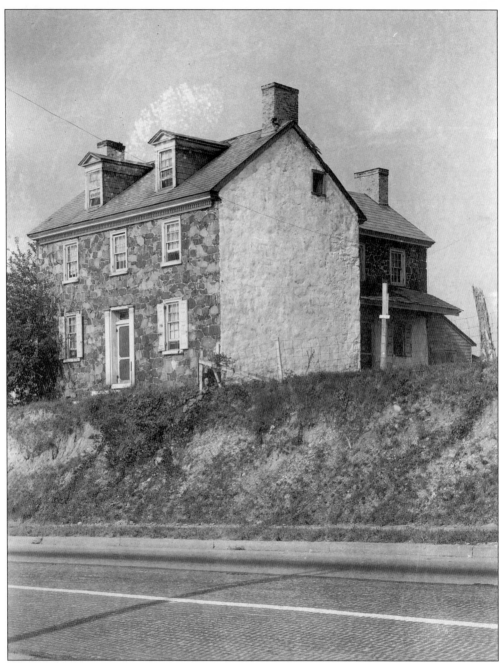

The home of William C. Lodge was located on the west side of the Pike opposite Rolling Park. The front portion was built around 1700 and the back was added around 1800. It was demolished in 1949 when Philadelphia Pike was widened. William C. Lodge was instrumental in the founding of the Church of the Ascension. William's three children, George, Anne, and Blanche, were born in this home. Anne married Thomas Parish and the couple, both artists, moved to Colorado Springs, CO. Anne eventually returned to Claymont with her two children, Anne and Dilwyn, who became writers and illustrators.

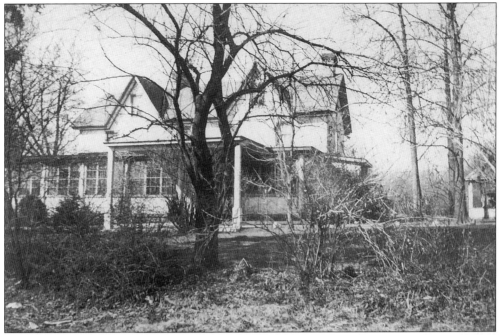

This home, built before 1868 and variously known as Maple Lane Inn, manor Inn, and Blue Manor Inn, was the home of William P. Lodge. Around 1900 it became the home of Robert Baldwin, who owned the Claymont Store when it stood at the present entrance to Archmere. In the 1920s, Blue Manor Inn was a popular "speakeasy."

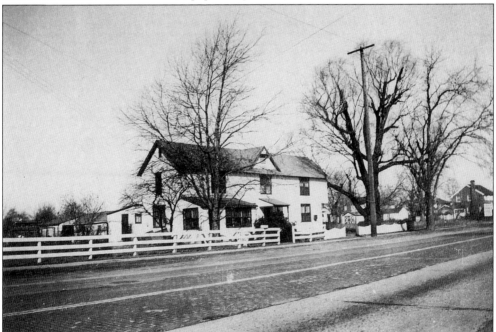

Originally owned by George Lodge, this was home to several black families. One resident was Everett James. The house was located on the west side of Philadelphia Pike at the head of Lodges Lane.

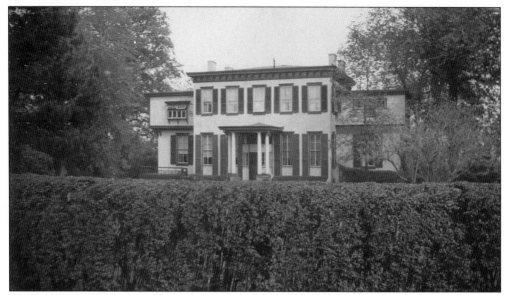

This house, built around 1840, was known as the Lodge-Parish House. It was located on the east side of Philadelphia Pike and was torn down in 1973 to make way for the WSFS Operations Center. George Lodge, a lawyer, lived here. After returning from Colorado, his sister, Anne Parish, and her children lived here. Anne's daughter, also named Anne, wrote many novels; among them *Tomorrow Morning*, *Golden Wedding*, *Methodist Fawn*, and the Harper's Prize–winning *The Perennial Bachelor*, which was about her uncle George. Her 1928 novel, *All Kneeling*, was made into the movie *Born to be Bad*, starring Joan Fontaine. She also wrote *We Were Three*, about her childhood in this house. Her reason for writing the book was so her children "would find the reason why I have never been successful in growing old."

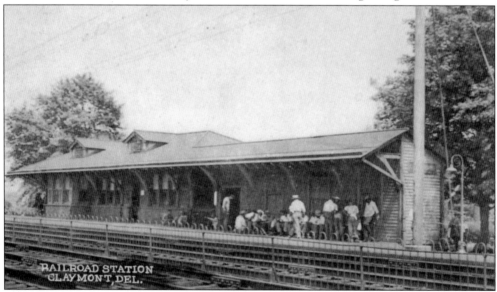

The Claymont Railroad station at the foot of Manor Avenue is shown here. Built in 1905 after the rail was rerouted in 1901, it was located to the east of the Worth Steel site along the Delaware River. The original station was built around 1838 at Naaman's Creek where CitiSteel is today. (Courtesy Schier Collection and Alan Barrowcliff.)

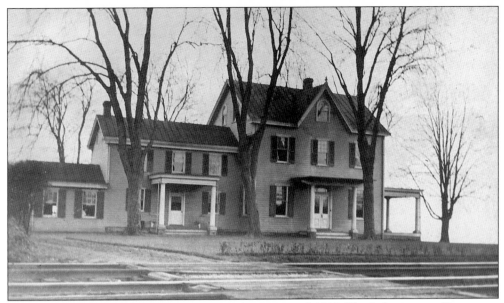

This is the "land side" of the Young House, shown around 1910. The left portion of house was built around 1735 and the right side was constructed around 1775.

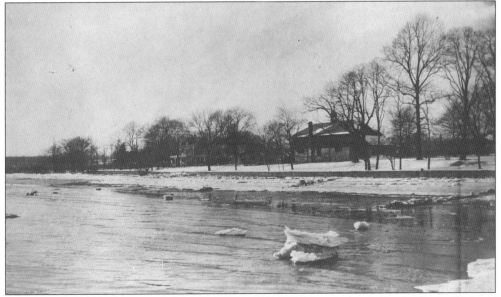

The Delaware River, looking south from the present railroad station at the foot of Manor Avenue, is shown here around 1910. On the left is the residence of Thomas Young. Prior to 1878, this was the farm of J. Hillborn Jones. The tenant house is visible in the center. To the right is the barn on the property of Gen. Isac Wistar, vice president of the Pennsylvania Railroad. These were all bought by the railroad and demolished to avoid rail crossing deaths.

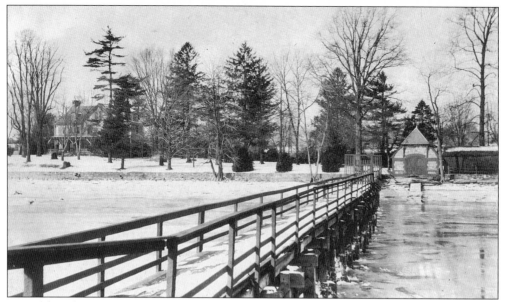

Pictured in this photograph is the residence of Gen. Isac Wistar, located at the foot of Shell Road (Governor Printz Road). The boat dock is to the right. When the house was torn down in 1929, the stone was used to build the home of Norman Jackson on Manor Avenue. Mr. Jackson was the station master at that time.

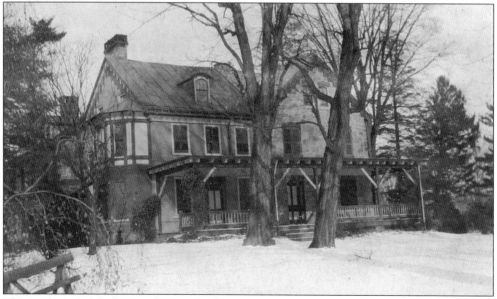

The south end of the home of General Wistar was made of English brick. The second floor had an imbedded cannon ball fired from the British sloop *Leopard* during the War of 1812. When the station was relocated in 1905, Wistar was responsible for getting it placed on the river side of the tracks for his convenience. This photograph was taken around 1910.

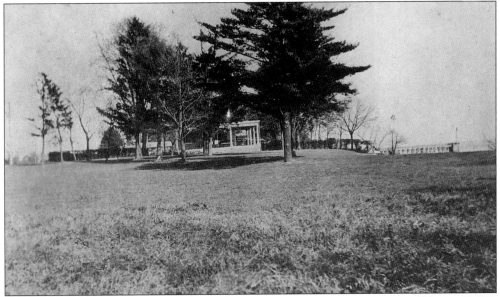

The residence of Thomas Young is shown here. To the right is General Wistar's pier. To the left of the Young House is the Wistar Green House.

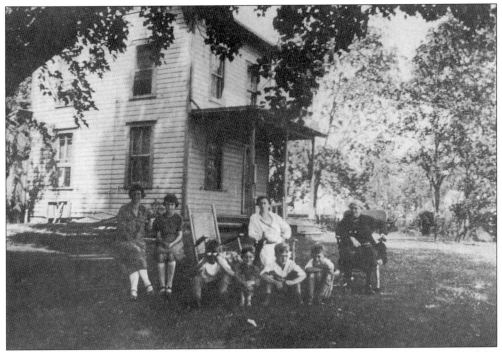

The station master's house for the Pennsylvania Railroad was located between the river and the 1905 station at the foot of Manor Avenue.

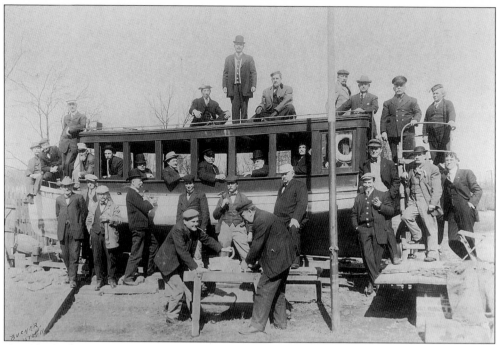

The Idle Hour Fishing Club members are shown on a yacht. The man in the front is painting the club's sign, which was a clock with the number "13" where "12" is supposed to go. This was the "idle hour." The club was located along the river just north of Grubbs Landing Road.

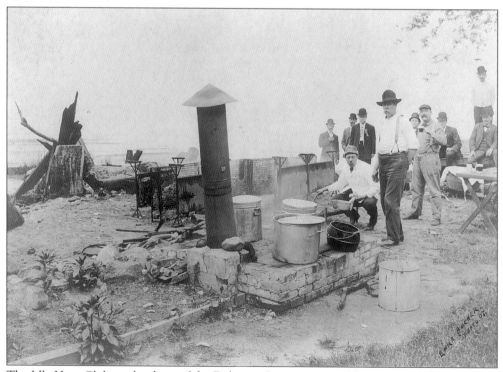

The Idle Hour Club on the shore of the Delaware River is pictured having a crab feast.

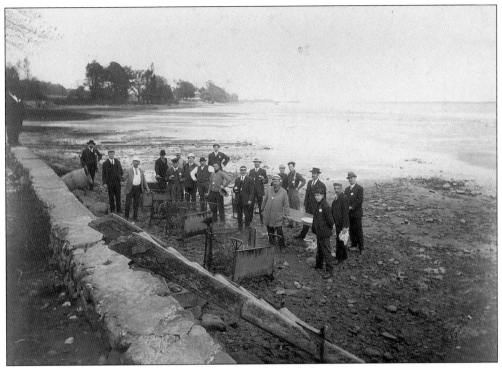

The Idle Hour Club had dinner on the Delaware River shore.

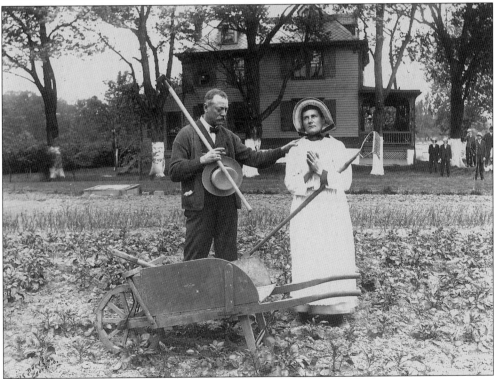

Members of the Idle Hour Club House are seen posing for a vignette.

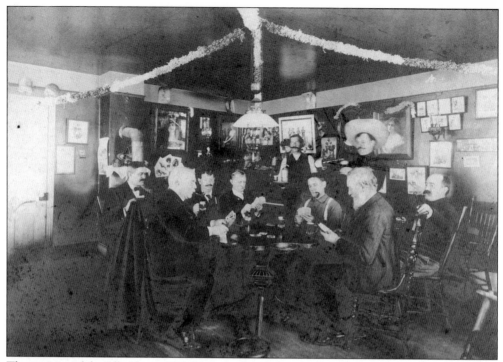

The interior of the Idle Hours Club House is shown here in the 1890s.

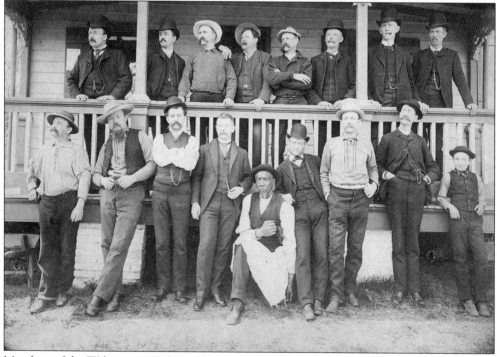

Members of the Wilmington Fishing Club are pictured here in 1888. Among those pictured are Coulton Johnson, Charles Thatcher, Duncan Thatcher, William Robelen I, ? McNiff, Harry Robelen, the cook, ? Adams, ? Hart, John Price, and William Robelen II.

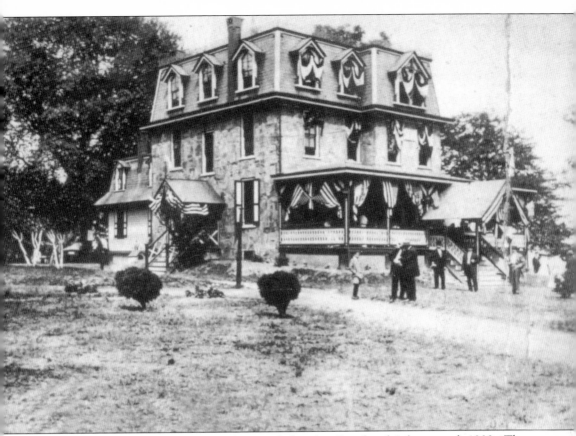

The Sangerbund House is shown decorated for the Fourth of July around 1900. The Sangerbund, later to become the Whistling Buoy, was originally the home of George Churchman, who owned the sawmill on Naaman's Creek. Located at the foot of Grubb's Landing Road, it became a popular fishing club in the late 1800s. During the 1920s, it was a popular speakeasy. The land, 150 acres, was assigned to John and Emanuel Grubb by Johnannes DeHaes in 1677. It developed into a popular shipping point along the Delaware River (Grubb's Landing). During the Revolutionary War, British troops landed here and on one occasion a cannonball shot from a sloop's deck hit the Practical Farmer Inn at the top of the hill.

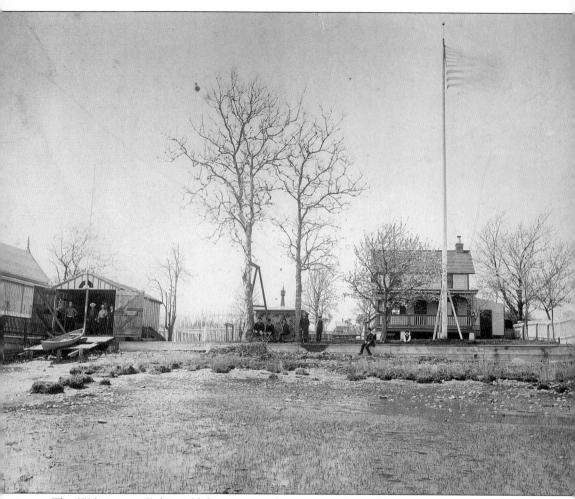

The Wilmington Fishing Club at Binstead is pictured here. Binstead was a group of houses located on the southeast edge of Claymont, between the railroad and the river. In the late 1800s and early 1900s, many of these homes became men's social clubs and sportsmen and fishing clubs.

The home of George and Maude Watterson, located at Binstead, is shown here around 1925. George Watterson was the last lightkeeper who tended the stationary shoal marker at Binstead. The light became electrified in 1925. (Courtesy of Mary Daller.)

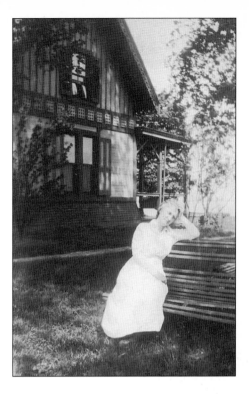

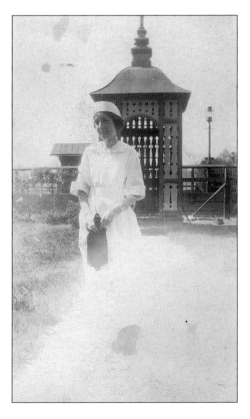

Louise Watterson in her nurses uniform is pictured here standing in front of the Victorian wellcover at the home of her parents, Maude and George. (Courtesy of Mary Daller.)

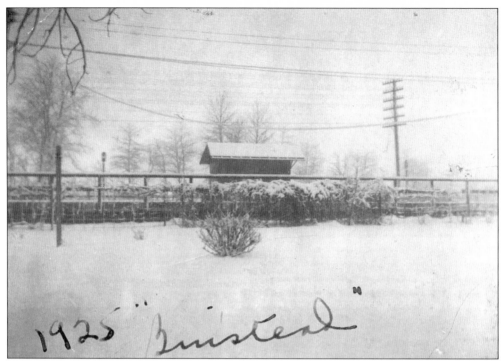

The Binstead Station was erected for George Lodge so he would have a convenient stop when he traveled to Philadelphia to study law. (Courtesy of Mary Daller.)

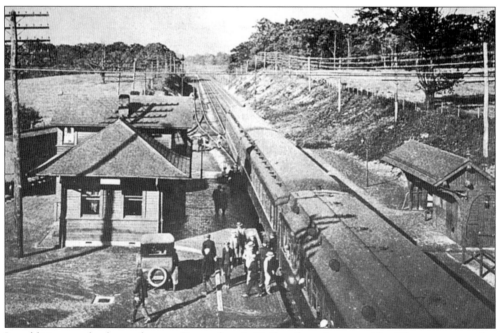

In addition to the better-known Pennsylvania Railroad on its east side, Claymont was also served by the B&O Railroad on its west side. Shown here is the Harvey Road Station, located on the south side of Harvey Road, east of the Ardens. (Courtesy of Bob Pyle.)

Three

CLAYMONT GROWS INTO THE 20TH CENTURY

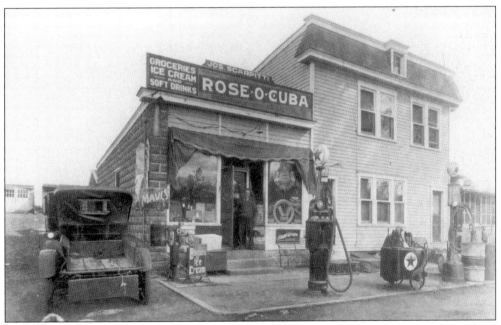

The Joseph Scarpitti Store, one of Claymont's early convenience stores, was located on Naaman's Road, between Philadelphia Pike and Ridge Road, just past the steel mill railroad tracks. The date of original building is unknown, but the house was added around 1915. The gas was hand-pumped and was 16.9¢. Mr. Scarpitti ran the commissary at Worth Steel prior to this store. (Courtesy of Pete Scarpitti Sr. and Al Scarpitti Sr.)

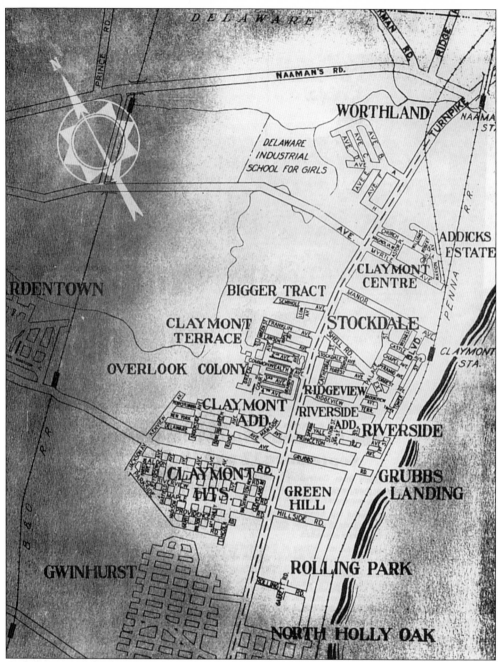

A street map of Claymont is shown here around 1948, before the Brookview Apartments and other key expansions had been built.

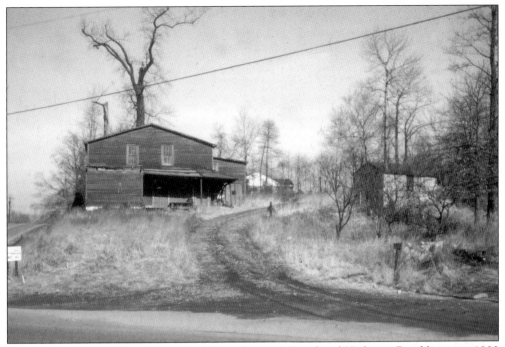

Vernon's Ice Cream Plant sat on the hill at Naaman's Road and Hickman Road between 1900 and 1940. This was a popular place for picnics in the early 1900s. This is also the site of the dueling grounds of the early 1800s.

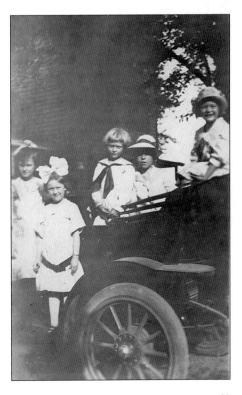

A Church of the Ascension Sunday School picnic to Vernon's Grove is shown here. The two children on the right are William G. Robelen II and Elizabeth Robelen.

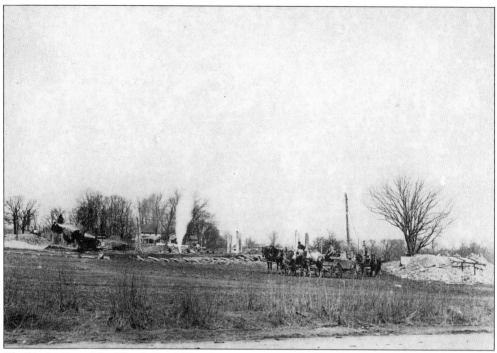

The beginning of the Worth Steel blast furnaces are pictured here around 1917 on the west side of Philadelphia Pike. The Marion Farmhouse is in the background.

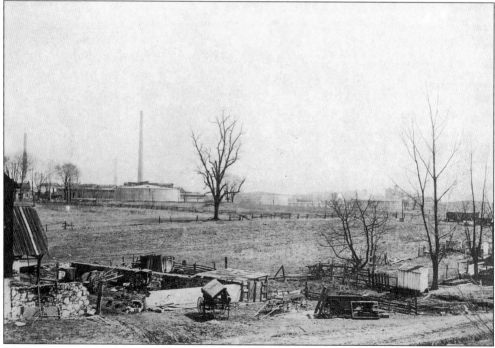

This is another 1917 scene of the Worth Steel construction. The road in the foreground was the lane that ran between Danzenbaker and the Graham homes down to the gristmill and sawmill along Naaman's Creek.

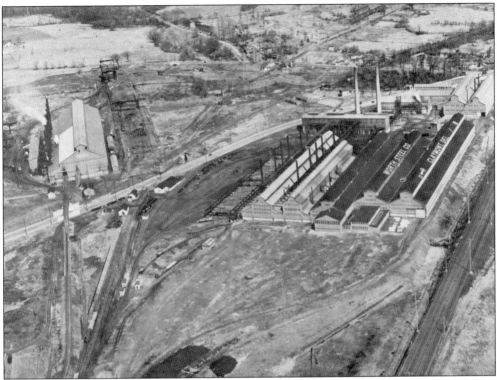

Worth Steel is shown here around 1945. The Robinson House is visible in the upper right. The Wertmüller House is near the end of the building that says "Claymont Delaware."

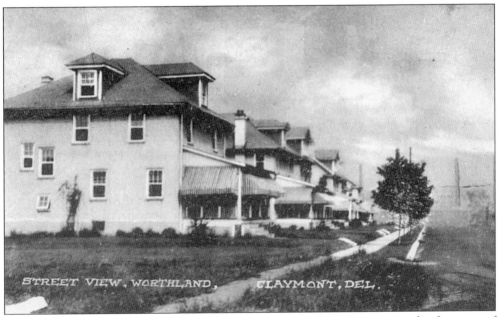

Worthland's superintendent's row on Avenue A, now Alcott Street, was the first row of housing in the company community. The hierarchy started with management in the first row, then went "down the line."

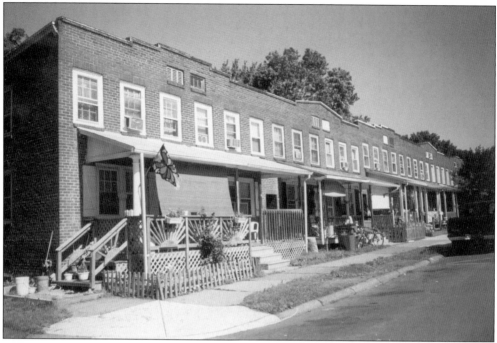

Pictured here are the homes on Avenue D at the rear of Worthland (now Denham Avenue, Knollwood). All the homes in Knollwood are privately owned and no longer the property of the steel plant.

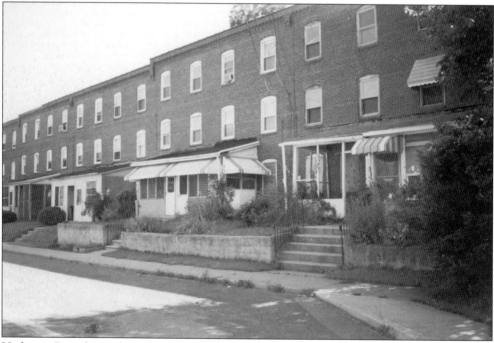

Hickman Row, located on Naaman's Creek Road, was built around 1917 by Worth Steel for their African-American employees. Like the homes of Worthland, they are still in use and are privately owned. (Courtesy of Ray Hester.)

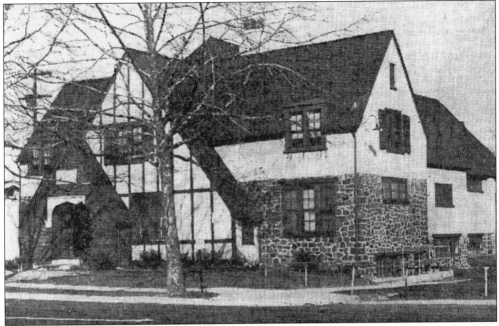

Worthland Clubhouse was built for the employees of Worth Steel. It contained a bowling alley, pool tables, and meeting rooms. It was the center for community gatherings. Later it was used by the Brandywine Lodge of the Masons.

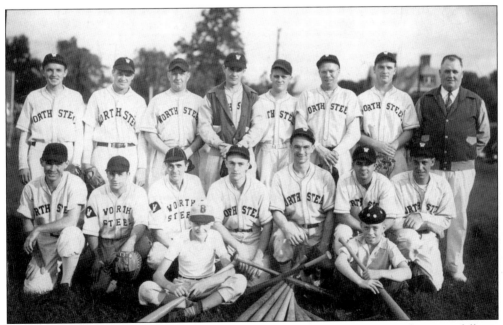

These members of the 1945 Worthland community ball team, from left to right, are as follows: (front row) Bub Tobin (second), Frankie Rumar (fifth), and Ivan Seaverson (sixth); (back row) Rip Oberly (second), Bill Oberly (fifth), John Appleton (sixth), Abby Short (seventh), and Al Oberly (eighth). John Appleton quit the Pennsylvania Railroad to come to Worth Steel so he could play on the team. (Courtesy of John S. Appleton Jr.)

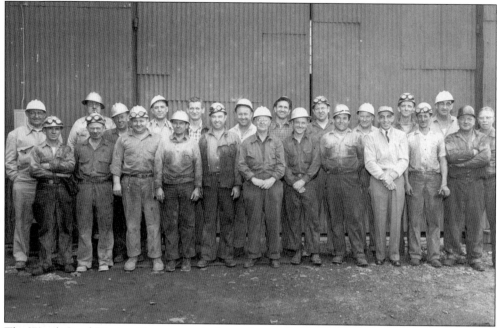

The Worth Steel Rigging Department is shown here. Mr. John Appleton is the second from the left. The team's manager had seen Mr. Appleton play ball and convinced him to take a job with Worth Steel so he could play on his team. (Courtesy of John S. Appleton Jr.)

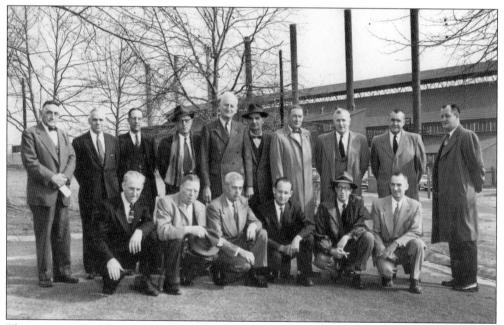

This is a picture of the managers of the Colorado Fuel & Iron Corporation around 1956. Shown here, from left to right, are the following: (first row) Ernie Hanthorne (elect. supt.), John Appleton (mechanical supt.), and Otis Swisler (lawyer); (second row) Mr. Maxwell (personnel), three unidentified men, and Mr. Wehrheim (housing director). (Courtesy of John S. Appleton Jr.)

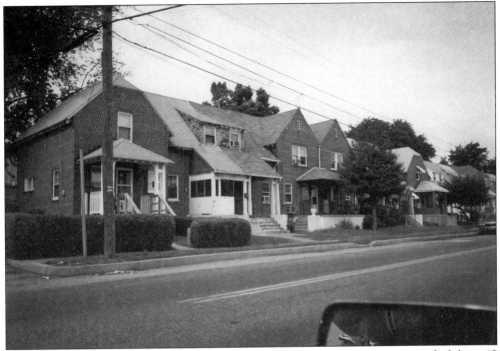

Aniline Village, the company housing of the National Aniline Company, consisted of about 40 townhomes on Ridge Road between Naaman's Road and the Pennsylvania state line. Some of the homes were in Pennsylvania. The buildings are still in use today and are now privately owned, as other company housing communities are.

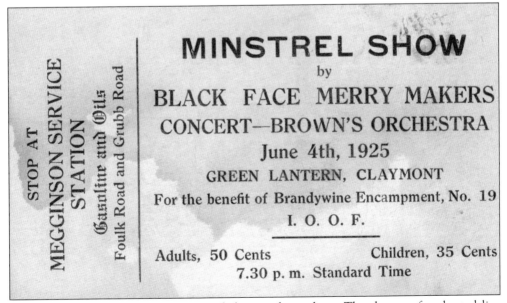

STOP AT
MEGGINSON SERVICE
STATION
Gasoline and Oils
Foulk Road and Grubb Road

MINSTREL SHOW
by
BLACK FACE MERRY MAKERS
CONCERT—BROWN'S ORCHESTRA
June 4th, 1925
GREEN LANTERN, CLAYMONT
For the benefit of Brandywine Encampment, No. 19
I. O. O. F.

Adults, 50 Cents   Children, 35 Cents
7.30 p. m. Standard Time

A ticket from a Green Lantern minstrel show is shown here. The theater often hosted live shows and concerts.

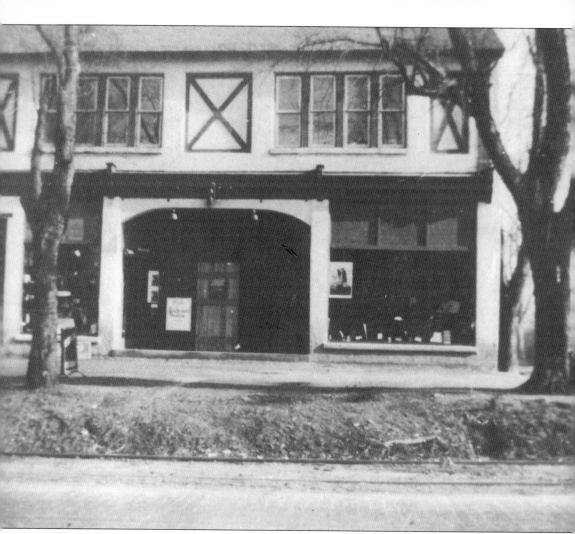

This is the Green Lantern Theater, which was built in 1920. It was located on the northeast corner of Myrtle Avenue and Philadelphia Pike, and was originally owned by George Lodge. Mr. Bill Habbert Jr. sold the tickets, Dorothy Talley played the piano, and Mr. Lodge collected the tickets. In the 1940s, Dick Edge owned the theater and ran contests for the children to dress in the costume of their favorite film heroes. If a kid did not have the nickel for admission, you could pretend you lost your money and Mr. Edge would "find" a nickel for you. During its life, the building was a silent movie theater, dance hall, recreation hall, and a church. It was demolished in 1972 to make way for a service station.

The Green Lantern Theater is shown here in the early 1950s after it had become Pike Theater and then Bible Baptist Church.

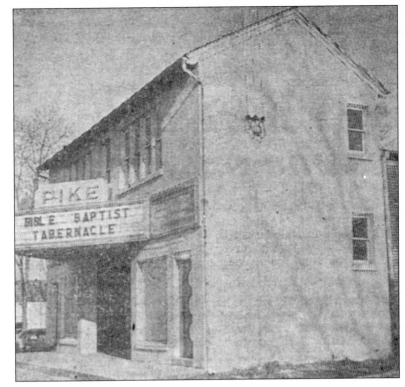

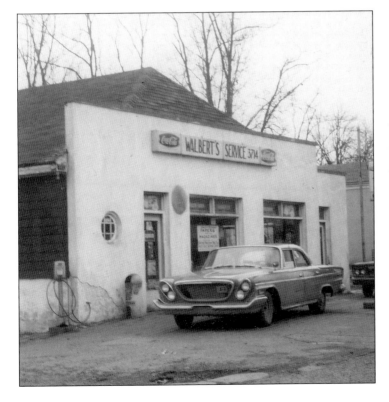

Walbert's Store, originally located in the Green Lantern Theater building, moved next door and became a filling station and a popular place for school kids to get penny candy, cold sodas, ice cream cones, bread, and milk. The location was between what became Dr. Schiek's dentist office (Dr. Jacobs today) and the Exxon station on the Pike just north of Myrtle Avenue.

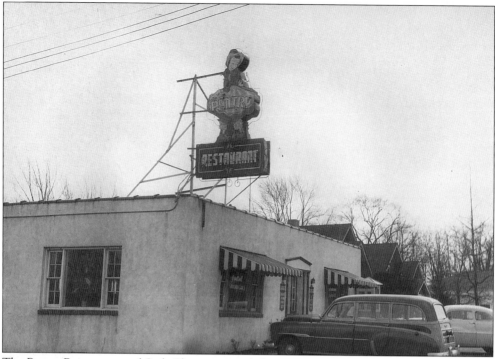

The Pantry Restaurant and Soda Shop was a popular teen spot operated by the Govatos family in the 1940s and 1950s. It was located on Philadelphia Pike at Church Lane and is now the two-story Fantini's Real Estate Office. (Courtesy of Ruth Govatos Stein.)

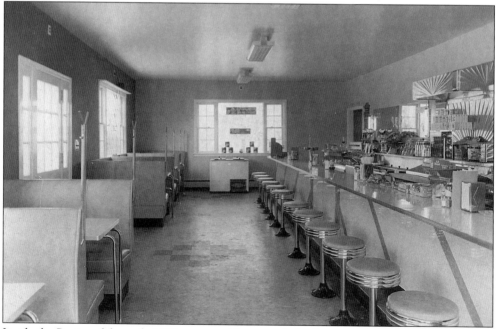

Inside the Pantry of the early 1950s, you could get a soda for 5¢, ice cream soda or milkshake for 20¢, cheeseburger for 30¢, and a T-Bone steak dinner, complete with a potato and salad, for $2. (Courtesy of Ruth Govatos Stein.)

Constant and Helen Mae Govatos, proprietors of the Pantry Restaurant, are shown here with their three children. The children, from left to right, are Ruthmargo, James, and George. (Courtesy of Ruth Govatos Stein.)

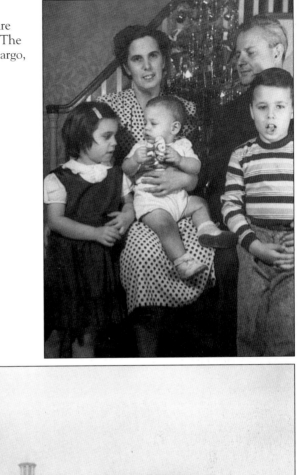

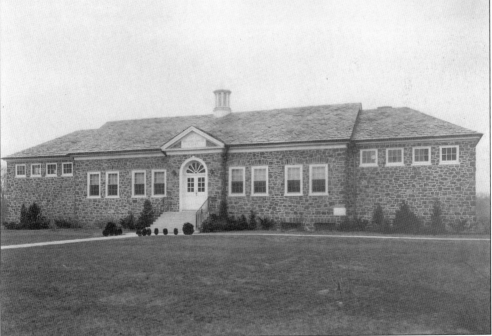

The Delaware Industrial School for Girls moved to Darley Road from Wilmington in 1917. Pictured here is the Phoebe Curtis Building. It was one of three key buildings erected for the school in order to "provide scholastic and skilled training for wayward girls." (Courtesy of the Historical Society of Delaware.)

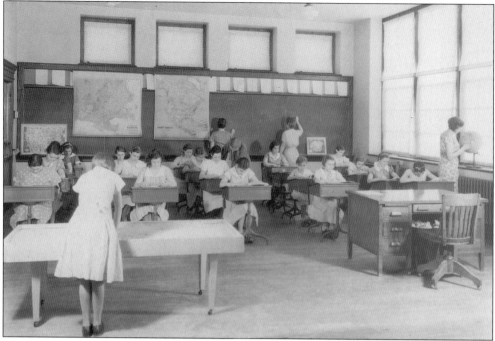

This classroom scene from the Delaware Industrial School for Girls was taken in 1934. (Courtesy of the Historical Society of Delaware.)

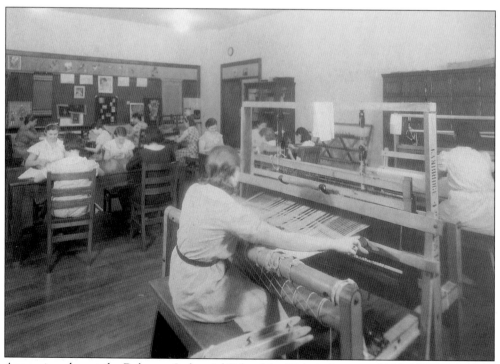

A weaving class at the Delaware Industrial School for Girls is shown in 1934. (Courtesy of the Historical Society of Delaware.)

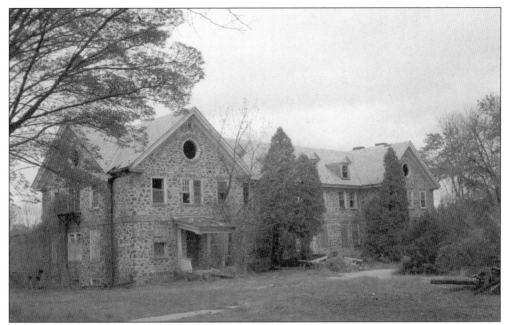

The Elizabeth C. Marks Building of the Delaware Industrial School for Girls (Woodshaven Kruse) is pictured here after vandalism occurred in the 1990s. This building has a fake 1893 cornerstone based on information that the school was started in Wilmington at that date and did not move to Claymont until later. (Courtesy of Theresa Fennick.)

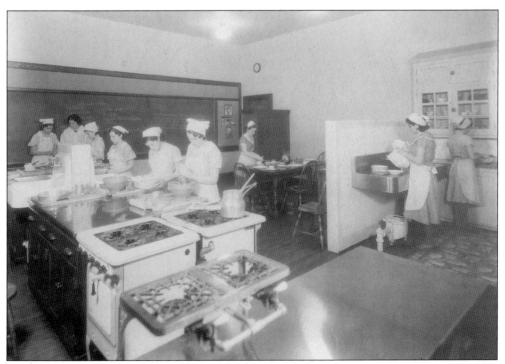

A cooking class at the Delaware Industrial School for Girls is shown in 1934. (Courtesy of the Historical Society of Delaware.)

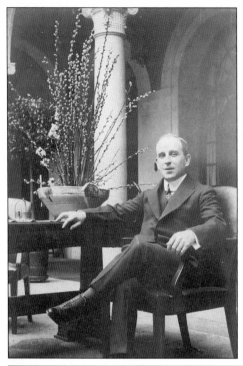

Mr. John Jacob Raskob, born in 1879, is shown here around 1925. Mr. Raskob was treasurer of the DuPont Company and headed General Motors. In 1928, while chairman of the National Democratic Committee, he managed the presidential campaign of Al Smith. Mr.Raskob also headed the syndicate that built the Empire State Building. He retired to Maryland, where he died in 1950.

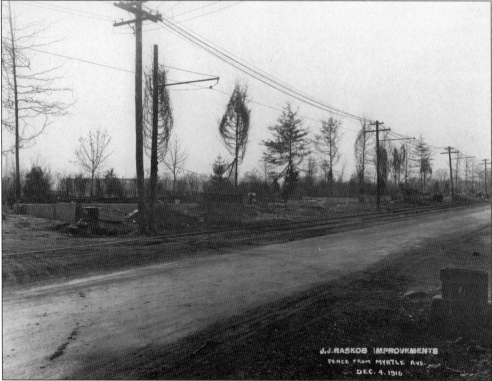

J.J. RASKOB IMPROVEMENTS
FENCE FROM MYRTLE AVE.
DEC. 4, 1910

Archmere construction at Philadelphia Pike and Myrtle Avenue is shown here. The trolley tracks are in the foreground of the fence. Note that in this 1916 photo the Pike is not yet paved.

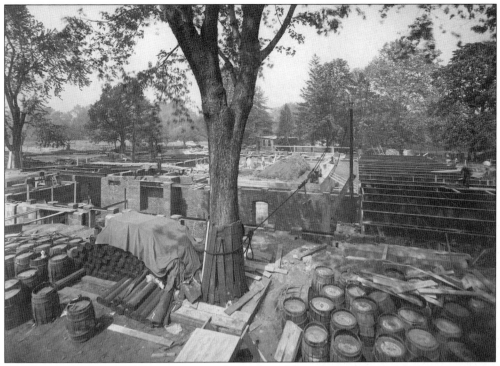

Another Archmere construction scene is shown here. Note the barrels of nails.

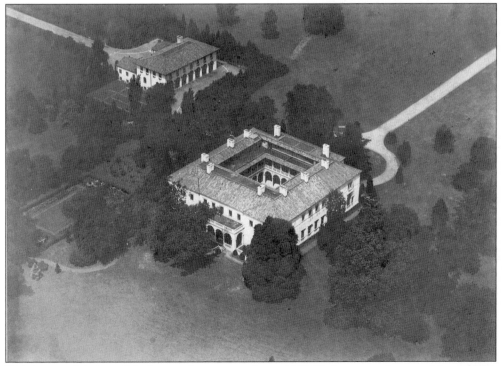

This is an aerial view of Archmere that appeared on a 1928 Christmas card sent to Mr. and Mrs. William G. Robelen II of Myrtle Avenue.

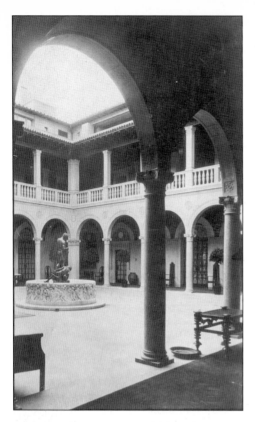

The Archmere courtyard is pictured here with its fountain. The fountain was commissioned by Mr. Raskob and the images of his 13 children are around the fountain's base.

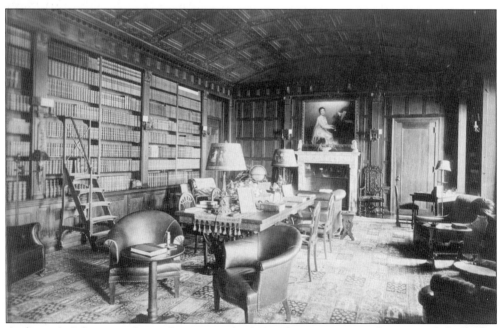

Archmere's Library is shown here around 1930. The portrait is of Mrs. Raskob (Helen S. Green).

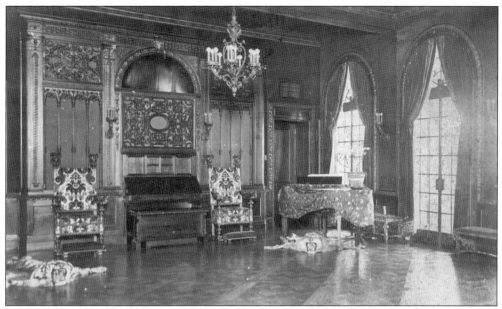

Archmere's music room is shown here around 1930. Note the organ.

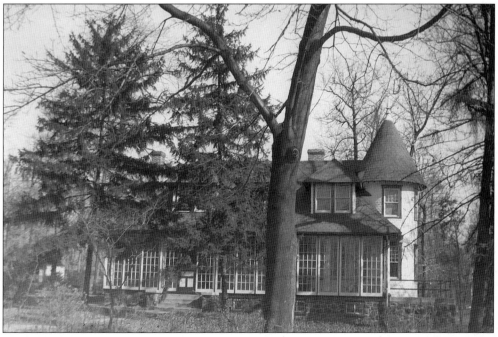

This was the original summer home of Charles Kurtz, though it was later bought by John Raskob and used for staff housing. It began as a bungalow, but then a tower and a large living room were added. Archmere used this as a "Senior's House" for a period. It was torn down for the construction I-495.

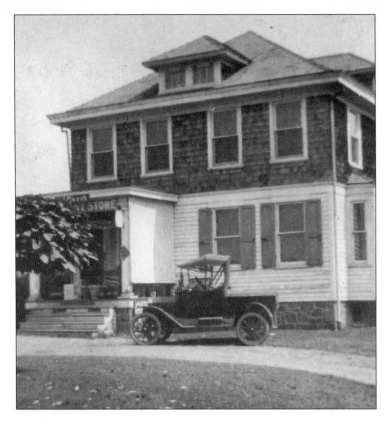

The Claymont Store in its original location on Philadelphia Pike at the main entrance to Archmere is shown here. It was moved across the street in 1917 by J.J. Raskob to make way for the gate to Archmere.

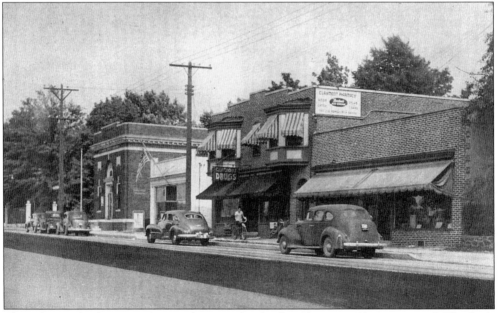

This photo of Claymont Center features the bank, Claymont Pharmacy, and Fletcher's Cleaners.

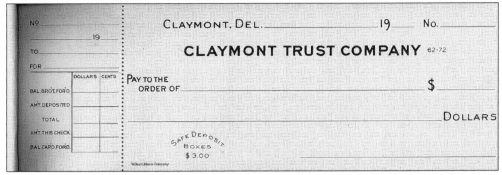

A check book from the Claymont Trust Bank is shown here.

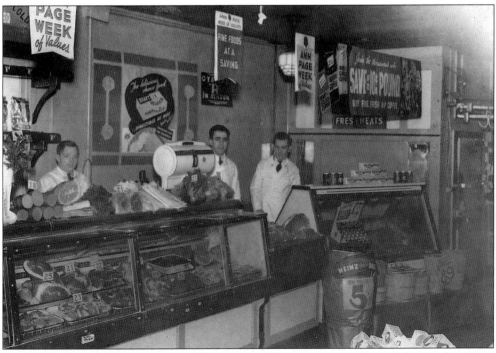

Pictured here is the interior of the Claymont A&P meat counter. From left to right are an unidentified man, Henry Casiato, and Al Wentz. The photo was taken by Robert G. Crump, a driver and salesman for the Wilmington Provision Company around 1940. (Courtesy of Alma J. Crump.)

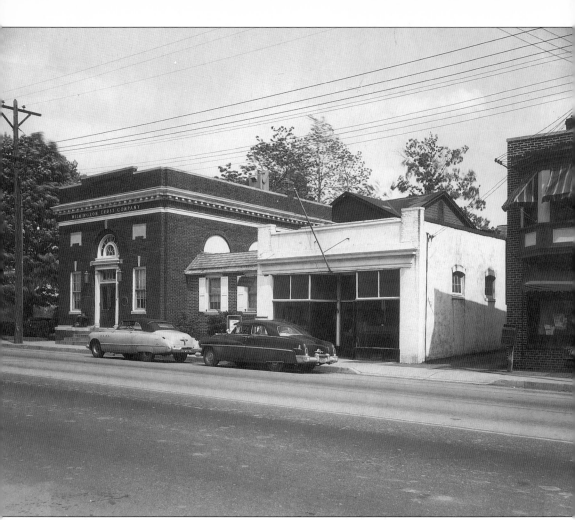

The Claymont Center is shown in this photograph from 1952. From left to right are the Wilmington Trust Bank, the post office, and the drug store. On September 8, 1923, the Claymont Trust Company opened in the building that is the post office in this picture. In 1924, the Claymont Trust Company moved into the new building and in 1949 it merged with Wilmington Trust. The post office was operated out of the drug store building in 1923. In 1930, they moved into the old Claymont Trust Building (as shown in picture). The post office had been established in 1812, but its location at that time is unknown. In 1853, it moved into Naaman's railroad station building. In 1905, it moved to the foot of Manor Avenue along with the rail station. The year of 1921 saw the post office move to McClure's Drug Store on the Pike. In 1930, it relocated into the Claymont Trust Building, and in 1961 it moved to its present location.

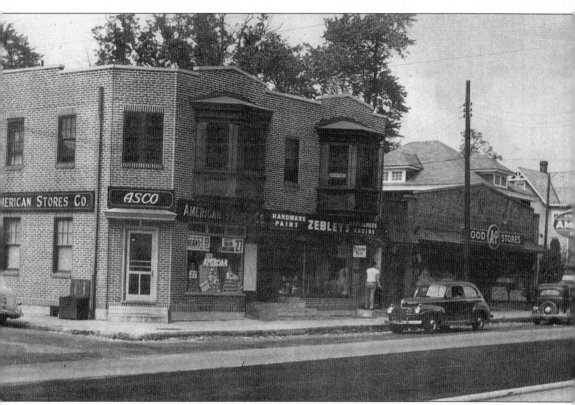

Claymont Center, located on the west side of Philadelphia Pike at Seminole Avenue, is pictured in this photograph from the 1940s. The American Store was later combined with Zebley's Hardware and made into the Richardson Variety Store. The A&P store remained here until it moved near Darley Road, where it became Superfresh Store in the late 1950s.

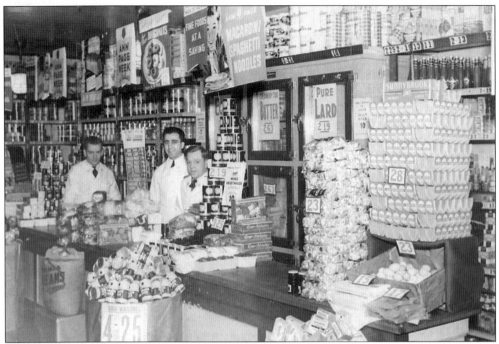

The Claymont A&P grocery counter is pictured here. Shown in this photograph taken by Mr. Crump, from left to right, are Al Wentz, Henry Casciato, and unidentified. (Courtesy of Alma J. Crump.)

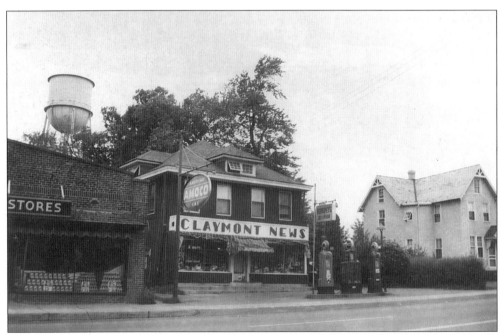

The Claymont News was also known as Buffington's Store. Buffington's daughter married Mike Wilson and they later operated the store. To the right can be seen the Atonement Methodist Church Parish House before it was torn down.

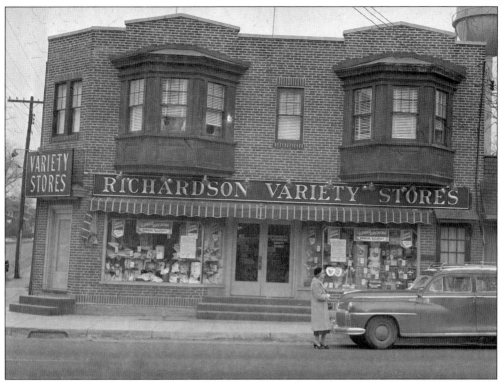

The Richardson Variety Store was located in Claymont Center in the 1940s at the corner of Seminole Avenue and Philadelphia Pike. From the 1940s through the early 1960s, it was one of six of the D'Iorio's stores. The store's name came from Richardson Park of southeast Wilmington. Mr. D'Iorio said that when he started his chain, he was concerned about prejudice against Italians due to the war raging in Europe at the time, so he chose the community's name instead of his own. Mr. D'Iorio related this story just a week before his passing at age 85 at his home near Claymont. (Courtesy of Teresa D'Iorio.)

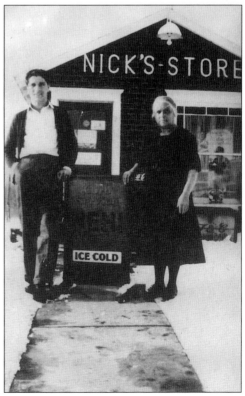

This is Nick's Store at Green Street and Commonwealth. The original store started in the house's garage around 1934. On the left is Joe Erace, Nick DiPinto's brother-in-law. Mary Nina DiPinto is pictured on the right. The senior Mr. DiPinto was born in Italy and came to America to be with his father, who worked for Worth Steel. He married Lena Erace from Philadelphia. (Courtesy of Nick and Lena DiPinto and sons.)

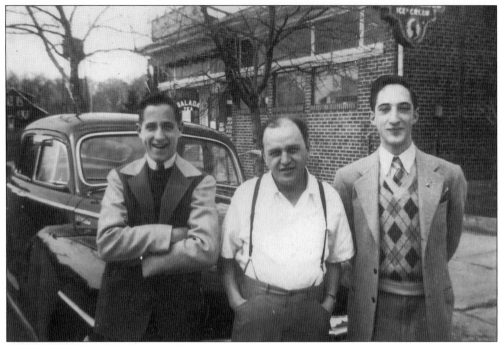

The second Nick's Store, built adjacent to the garage and onto the house around 1946, is pictured here. From left to right are Joe DiPinto, Lardear DiPinto, and Anthony DiPinto. Nick's Store was always a popular spot, being just down the street from the school. Nick Sr. had borrowed $65 from his brother-in-law to start the original store. His sons are Anthony, Joe, and Nick Jr. (Courtesy of Nick and Lena DiPinto and sons.)

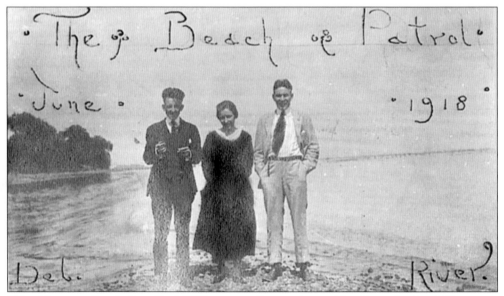

"The Claymont Beach Patrol" of 1928 are actually members of the Casey family of Claymont. Pictured on the shore of the Delaware River near the foot of Manor Avenue, from left to right, are Paul Taqarty, Cora Casey (Jim Rambo's grandmother), and Harold Pituro. (Courtesy of Linda K. Rambo.)

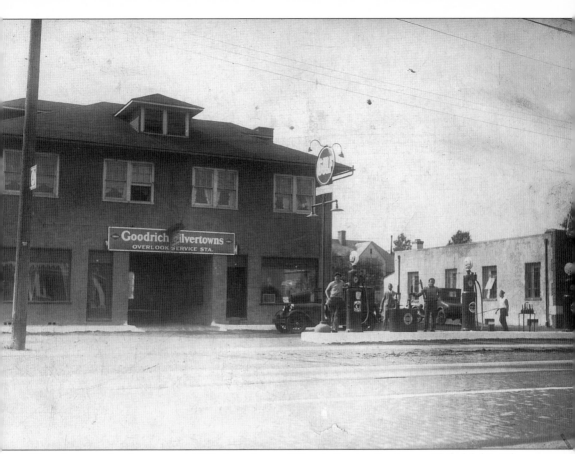

This photograph taken around 1930 shows Joe and Tony's Service Station on Philadelphia Pike at Overlook Colony, which was operated by the Vassalotti Brothers from 1948 to 1967 and was purchased by Mike DeCostanza in 1967. Built around 1928, it was a Studebaker show room in the 1930s and still operates today as a service station and auto repair place under owners John and Mike DeCostanza. According to the Gulf Oil Company, it is the longest continuous operating Gulf station in America. John and Mike received the New Castle County's Historic Review Board's "Preservation Award" in 2000. (Courtesy of John and Mike DeCostanza.)

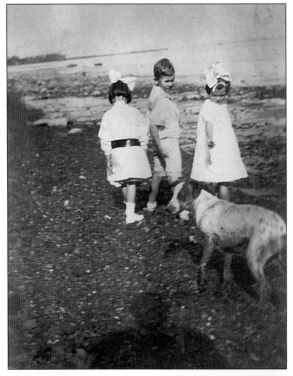

The Robelen family enjoys an outing to the beach along the Delaware River at the foot of Myrtle Avenue. From left to right are Margaret Baker, William G. Robelen II, Elizabeth Robelen, and Towser (the dog).

"We found the peaches" was the cry of William G. Robelen II (with shovel) in the yard of his Myrtle Avenue home. It was a common practice to put peaches in a jar with brandy and bury it for about a year. From left to right are Lillian Robelen, Theodore Rosin, W.G. Robelen II, and his sister, Elsie Robelen Rosen. Ms. Rosen was a suffragette, and was one of those who chained themselves to the White House fence.

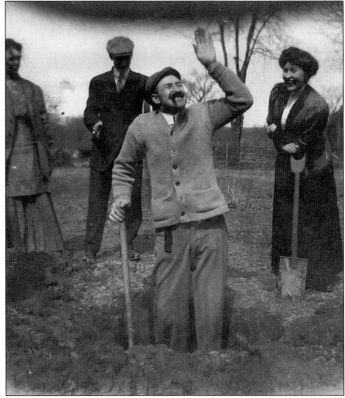

Harvey Stahl, shown here in 1940, was the first superintendent of the Claymont public schools, serving from 1922 until 1955. One of his most notable roles, among many, was in the integration of Claymont High School. In 1952, the Delaware Department of Education ordered Mr. Stahl to "send the colored children home." Mr. Stahl refused to do so, saying that "we're dealing with the lives of children here." The school board backed Mr. Stahl's decision and the students stayed and were quietly accepted. (Courtesy of Miriam Stahl.)

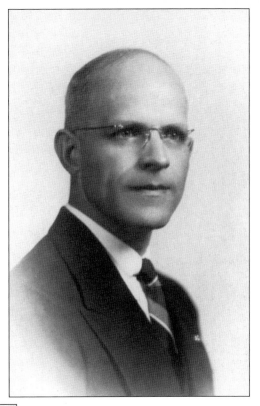

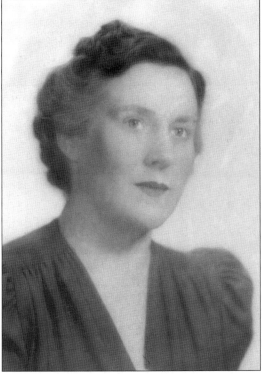

Mrs. Miriam Stahl married Harvey Stahl on June 29, 1940. She graduated from the University of Pennsylvania and Temple University and taught in the Philadelphia schools for 38 years. She was a founding member of the Delaware and Claymont chapters of AARP and served as state director for 4 years. Today, she remains active at age 98, living in Greenville, DE. (Courtesy of Miriam Stahl.)

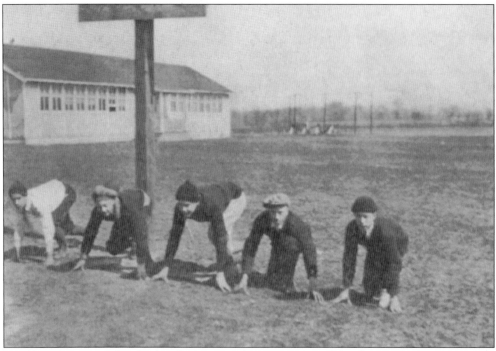

Franklin Avenue School, also known as the Tar Paper School, was built in 1920 to accommodate the growth brought about by the rapid expansions in local industry.

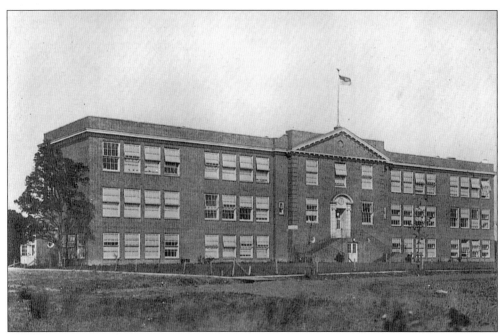

The Claymont High School is shown here in 1928. (Courtesy of the Claymont High School Alumni Association.)

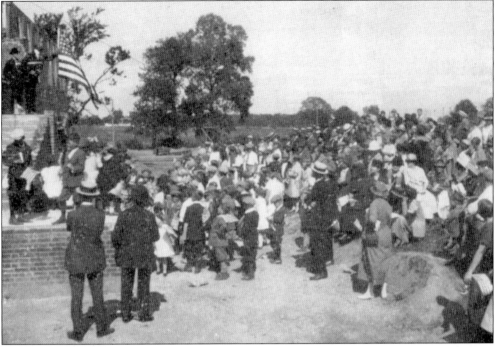

The laying of the cornerstone for Claymont High School is visible in this picture dating back to September 6, 1924. The main speaker was Harvey Stahl. The school served students from grades 1 through 12. The Naaman's School (Old Stone School) continued to serve kindergarten students into the early 1950s. (Courtesy of Miriam Stahl.)

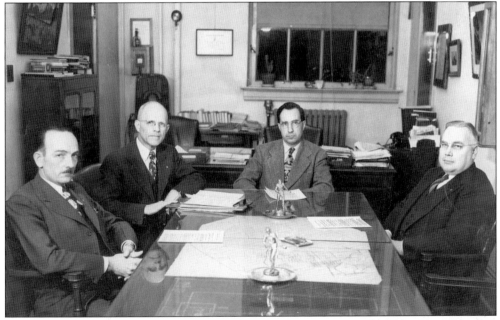

This is a 1948 picture of the Claymont Special School District's Board of Education. From left to right are A.A. Fletcher, H.E. Stahl, M.A. Dietrich (board president), and M.A. Penneg. (Courtesy of Joyce R. Breeding Light.)

GRADUATING CLASS OF '29

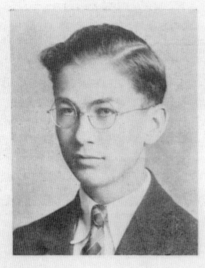

HERBERT GEORGE McWALTER

"In youth and beauty wisdom is but rare."

Sports Editor of CLAY TABLET, I, IV; Class Monitor, I, II, III; Editor-in-Chief of CLAY TABLET, II, III; Vice-President of Sportsmanship Brotherhood, II; Member of Basketball Team, II, IV; Captain of Basketball Team; Secretary of Class II; President of Athletic Association, III, IV; President of Sportsmanship Brotherhood, III; President of Science Club, III; Captain of Volleyball Team, III, IV; Member of School Soccer Team, III, IV; Honors in Oratorical Contest, III; First in School, Second in County, Honorable Mention in State, Second in Silver Medal Contest, First in Gold Medal; School Dramatics: Safety First" III, "In The Trenches Over There," III, "Apple Blossom Time" IV, Oratorical Contest, IV; First in County, First in School; Won Letter "C", III.

ALICE FRANCES GALVIN

"I am sober as a judge, Silence gives consent."

Substitute on Freshman Basketball Team, I; Won Bronze Badge, II; School Dramatics: "In the Trenches Over There" III; Class Monitor, III, IV; News Editor of CLAY TABLET, two editions, IV; Secretary of Class, IV; Secretary of Caesar Latin Class, IV; Member of Volleyball Team, IV; Member of Glee Club, I.

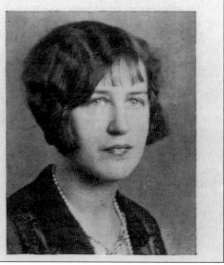

This is the first page of the first graduating class of Claymont High School in 1929. It comes from the 1929 *Clay Tablet*. (Courtesy of Evelyn McDaniel of the Claymont High School Alumni Association.)

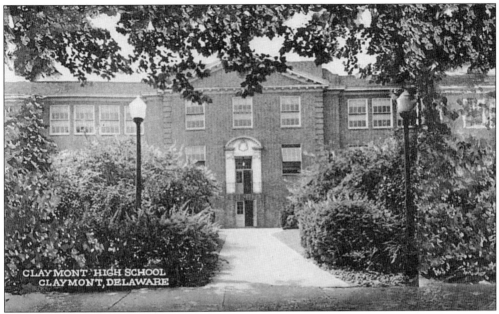

Claymont School is shown here in the 1940s with lots of shrubbery and street lights.

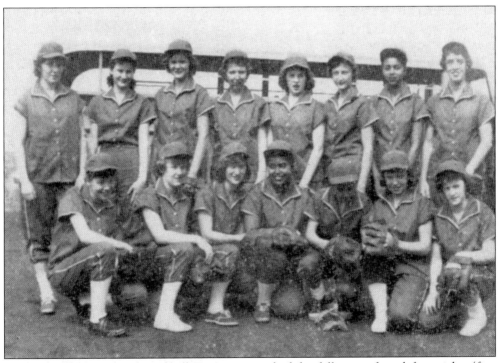

The 1955 Claymont High Softball Team consisted of the following, from left to right: (first row) A. Seagraves, B. Casey, J. Harper, C. Anderson, C. Lange, A. Duffy, and D. Jones; (second row) B. Murray, E. Gentieu, A. Welsh, B. Coulborne, C. Duffy, S. Mahla, J. Anderson, and S. Sylvester. (Courtesy of Miriam Stahl.)

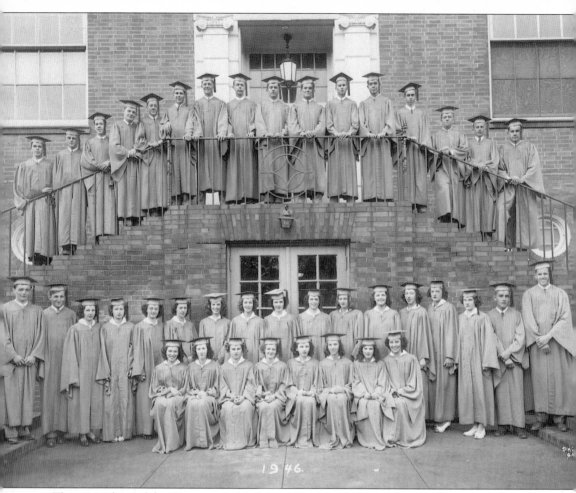

These members of the Claymont High School Graduating Class of 1946, shown here from left to right, are as follows: (first row) Gwen Thomas, Nancy Johnson, Anna Pyle, Betty Radcliffe, Doris Kirkley, Jane Potter, Ann Dougherty, and Olga Procyshyn; (second row) William Evans, Joseph Mechell, Helen Reid, Evelyn Parlier, Jean Hays, Eleanor Knapp, Esther Michener, Norma Perry, Audrey Perry, Ethelene Faircloth, Mary E. Carpenter, Shirley Moyse, Edythesites, Sally Stewart, Sophie Gebert, Joseph Parkinson, and William Casey; (third row) Donald Bennet, Robert Bierley, Hugh Garvin, Karl Cossaboon, Albert Cruciano, Clarence Kelley, Andrew Campbell, Llewellyn Withrow, Richard Smith, Archie Rapposelli, William Elder, Victor Fantini, Oather McDaniel, Ronald Macturk, John Ferry, and John Maslin.(Courtesy of Eleanor M. Burns (Knap), 1946 graduate and resident of Claymont for 72 years.)

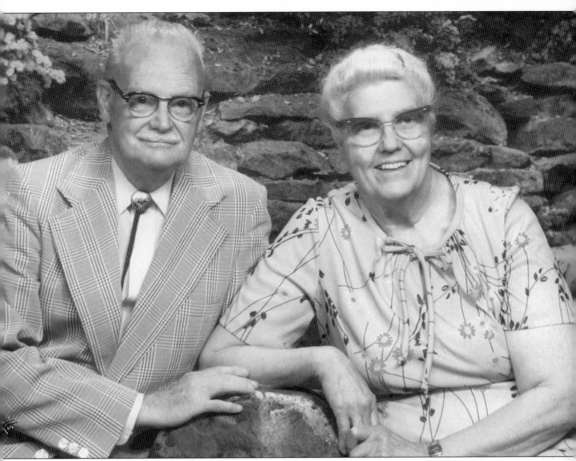

Sager "Doc" and Evelyn Tryon moved to Claymont in 1946. Dr. Tryon served on the Claymont School Board from 1950 until 1962, spearheading the move to integrate Claymont High School in 1952, two years before the U.S. Supreme Court's Brown decision. He was a primary founder, with Betty McMullen, of the Claymont Community Center and served the community through several organizations. Evelyn Tryon was the church organist at the Atonement Methodist Church for 30 years and taught math in the Wilmington schools. Together they served, after retiring, in the Peace Corps in the Fiji Islands from 1976 to 1978. After leaving Fiji, they traveled across Asia and then returned to Claymont and continued community service here. Sager died in 1988 and Evelyn remains active in the community, receiving the Founder's Award in recognition of her community service in 1997. (Courtesy of Evelyn and Ginny Tryon Smilack.)

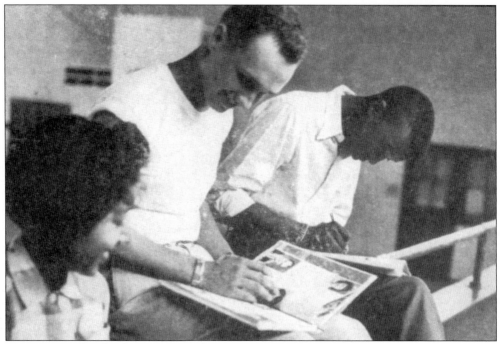

Claymont High School was integrated in 1952, prior to the Brown vs. the Board of Education U.S. Supreme Court decision. In a 1997 ceremony at the Claymont Community Center, Judge Collins J. Seitz, Mr. Tryon (former president of the Claymont Board of Education), Harvey Stahl (former superintendent of schools), high school students (black and white), and the Claymont community all were recognized for doing the right thing prior to being forced to by the Supreme Court. (Photo courtesy of Miriam Stahl; information courtesy of Evelyn Tryon and Ginny Tryon Smilack.)

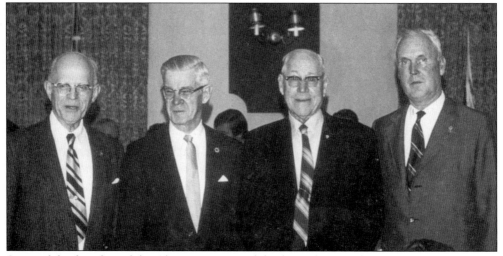

Some of the founders of the Claymont Lions Club, shown here in the 1940s, are, from left to right, Harvey Stahl (superintendent of schools), Frank Bourn (pharmacist and owner of the Claymont Pharmacy), George Bigger (plumber and founder of the Claymont Building and Loan), and Bill Jones (owner of Jones Funeral Home in Claymont, now Geibhart's). (Courtesy of Mrs. Miriam Stahl.)

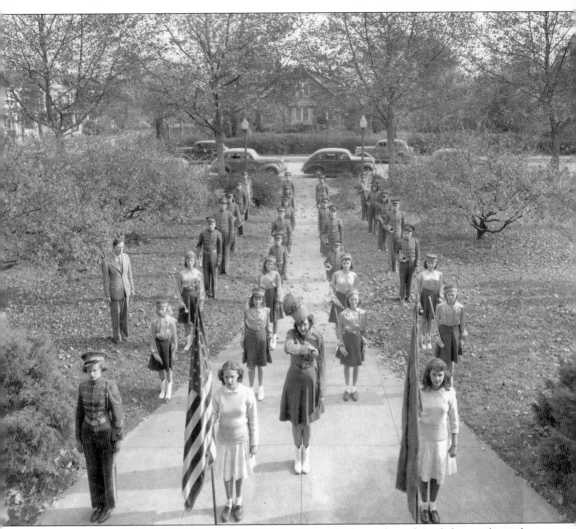

These members of the 1944 Claymont High School Band, shown here from left to right and front to back, are as follows: (first row) Jean White, Barbara Woodall, Audrey Hadfield, Robert Irwin, Russell Wainwright, Esther Michener, Wilfred Smith, and James McDaniel; (second row) Jane Carpenter, Lois Carpenter, Betty Wright, Richard Pinney, Lawrence Glaeser, Jane Banks, and Constance Lowther; (third row) Joan Smith, Joyce Breeding, Neil Thomas, Robert McDowell, Jean Stevens, Charles Dietrich, and Ethelene Faircloth; (fourth row) Anna Greigg, Anne Morgan, Marie Ruebeck, Donald Shepperly, Hugh Garvin, Doris Sheldon, Jean Hays, and Melvyn Farber. The majorette is Martha Palmer. (Courtesy of Joyce R. Breeding Light.)

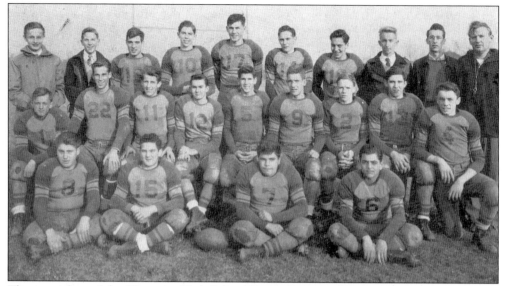

These members of the Claymont High School Football Team of 1943, shown here from left to right, are as follows: (first row) Wilbur Johnson, Archie Rapposelli, John Lardear, and Tom Saffo; (second row) Bob Bierley, Bob Jones, Warren James, Earle Marvel, Jug Elliott, Walt Abplanalp, Jim Dickinson, Ham Ford, and Arky Vaughan; (third row) Kenmore Schweitzer, Allen Snyder, George Callahan, Jack Morris, John Maslin, Dick Dickens, Norman McBride, Howard Husbands, Richard Onley, and Coach Russ Faber. (Courtesy of Grover "Jug" Elliott.)

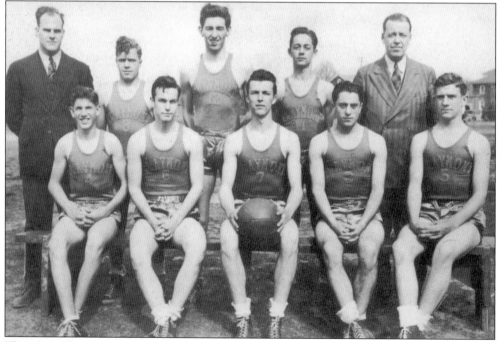

The 1942 Claymont High School Basketball Team poses for a photograph. From left to right are the following: (first row) Grover (Jug) Elliott, Philip Neff, Marvin Vernon, Louis Minutola (captain), and Walter Abplanalp; (standing) Coach Salisbury, Edwin Anderson, John Fannon, Albertus Waters, and Assistant Coach Taylor. (Courtesy of Grover "Jug" Elliott.)

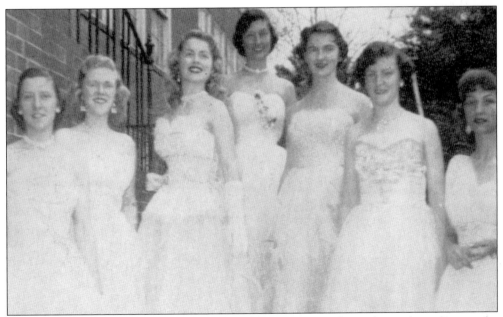

The 1942 Claymont High School Baseball Team included Walters, Neff, Elliott, Pyle, Abplanalp, Minutola, Jones, Vernon, Mechell, Lenox, and J. Ware. (Courtesy of Grover "Jug" Elliott.)

The Claymont High School May Queen and her court are shown here. According to the *Claymont Chanticleer*, "adding sparkle to the May Day festivities were the seven *demoiselles* . . ." Shown here, from left to right, are Hope Clothier, Carolyn Wolfe, Mollie Ann Bourn (lady-in-waiting), Bette Ann Conly (May queen), Nancy McDowell, Diane Jones, and Barbara Roberts. (Courtesy of Miriam Stahl.)

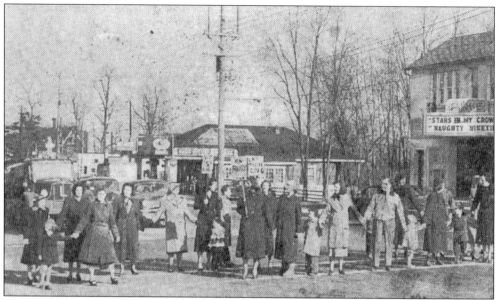

In 1953, there was no light at the corner of Philadelphia Pike and Darley Road at Old Stone School. The Claymont School Parent-Teacher Association took matters into their own hands and literally stopped traffic several days on the Pike until the state highway department agreed to install a traffic light. PTA President Herb C. Foote noted a two-year fight had transpired prior to the protest.

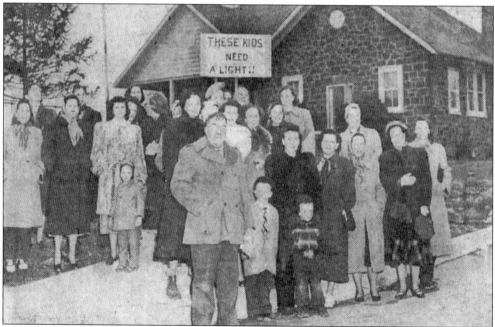

In 1953, parents of kindergarten children of the Naaman's School (Old Stone School) demonstrated for a stop light at Philadelphia Pike and Darley Road. Mr. Herbert C. Foote is the gentleman in front. He was chairman of the PTA Safety Committee. The demonstration was repeated morning and afternoon until the state highway department (now DELDOT) agreed to install the light. The 25 mph speed limit also was not being followed.

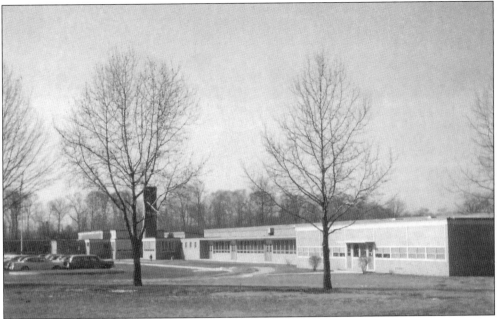

Green Street Elementary School was built in 1953 to accommodate the growing Claymont population. Its 25 classrooms were used by the students of the original elementary school, so the elementary school could serve a high school.

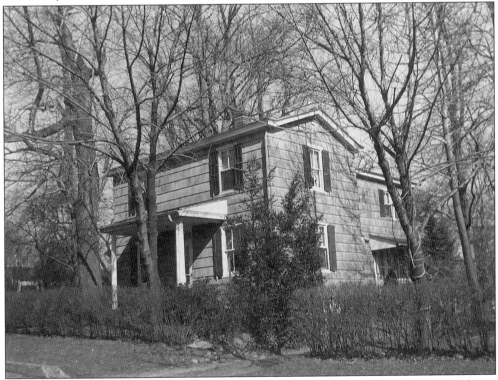

This was the home of Mr. and Mrs. Harvey Stahl on Manor Avenue. Mr. Stahl was superintendent of the Claymont Special School District from 1924 to 1955.

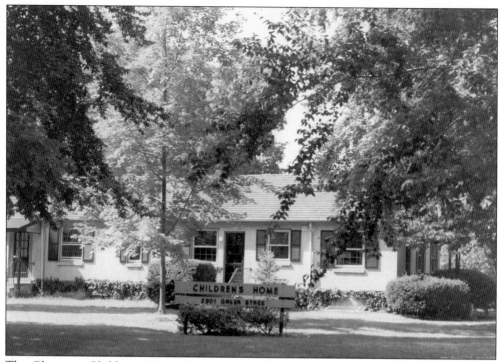

The Claymont Children's Home began in 1863 as The Home for Friendless and Destitute Children, on King Street in Wilmington. The name was changed and the home was moved to Claymont in 1948. It was located on a 14-acre plot, donated by Mr. and Mrs. Edward Worth, on Green Street, and had Claymont's first cottage, which was built in 1952. The Diocese of Wilmington/Catholic Charities became the owner in 1995. (Courtesy of The Children's Home, Claymont.)

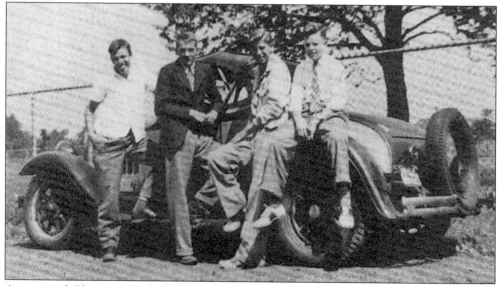

A group of Claymont High School students are seen "hanging out" with a late model Studebaker. Shown here, from left to right, are John Ware, Jimmy Ware, Dusty Rhodes, and Charles Dickerson. (Courtesy of Dusty Rhodes, now of Texas.)

Thomas A. Kellum, the first chief of the Claymont Fire Company, is pictured in this 1928 photograph. (Courtesy of Sam Kelly.)

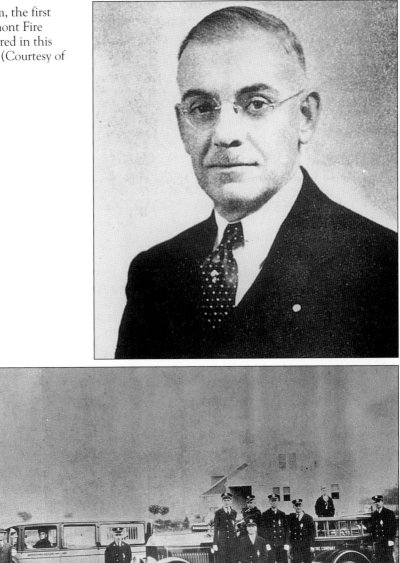

The Claymont Fire Company Number 1 is pictured here in 1929. On January 25, 1928, Joseph Tatnall called a meeting for the purpose of organizing a local volunteer fire company. About 300 residents became members and the Red Men's organization allowed them use of their hall in Overlook Colony. The first equipment was donated by the Overlook Public Service Association. On March 6, 1928, the company was called to its first drill. The company has served proudly ever since. (Courtesy of Sam Kelly.)

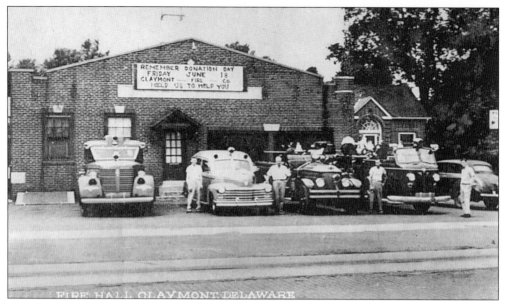

The original Claymont Fire Company building is shown here around 1949. Pictured, from left to right, are L. Pugh, Mike Wilson, George Casey, Les Carpenter, and Russell Whitman. This was the home of the fire company from 1928 to 1952. The building was bought by Bible Baptist Church and remodeled in 1954. After the original Claymont Fire Company came the Wilmington Suburban Water Co., then the fire company took the building back.

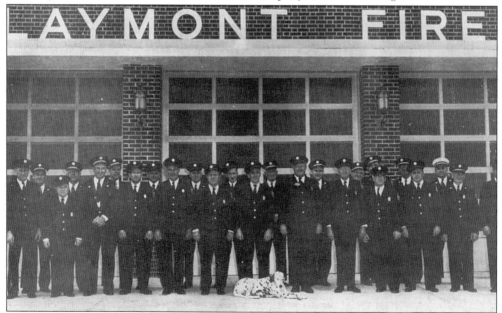

The Claymont Fire Company in 1954, including the dog Dell, is shown here. From left to right are Walter Wilson, Okie Thompson, Francis Crerand, Ellsworth Baker, Harry Peters, Edward Elliotte, Robert Bromall, Harry Temple, Edward Van Gordor Sr., Armond Duphilllly, Charles Brady, Glen Schumaker, John Casey, Charles Gurskie, Harvey Grant, Ralph Remington, William Hickman, Cecil Endecott, Edward Anderson Sr., Lee Murphy, William Jackson Sr., Walter Heal, Robert Hamilton, and Jack Webb.

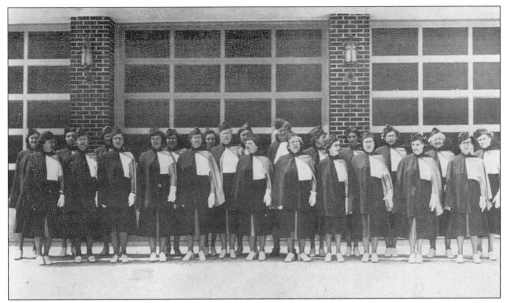

The Claymont Fire Company's Ladies Auxiliary is shown here at Dedication Day in 1954. From left to right are Mary Ellen Yerkie, Marie Mears, Katheerine Lawson, Mary MacNamara, Margaret Jackson, Mary Humble, Katherine Thompson, Rachel Clark, Nellie Murphy, Carol Elliott, Estelle Baker, May Robinson, Ruth VanGorder, Nellie Sakers, Gladis Hickman, Ellen Yerkie, Alta Remington, Alice Webb, Elizabeth Brady, Ann Hickey, Myrtle Peters, Etta Everhart, Lola Holbrook, Sarah Clark, and Wilhelmina Longmore.

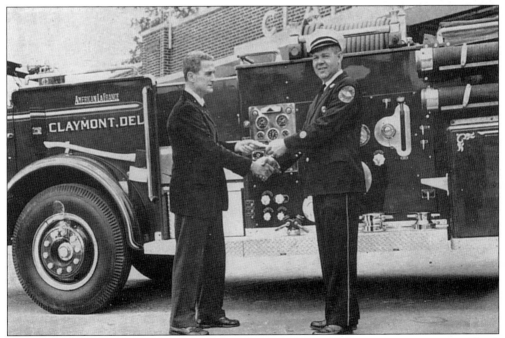

Daniel F. Harkins (right), president of the Claymont Lions Club, is seen presenting a check to Claymont Fire Company Chief Sam Kelly for a radio for the fire engine. (Courtesy of Sam Kelly.)

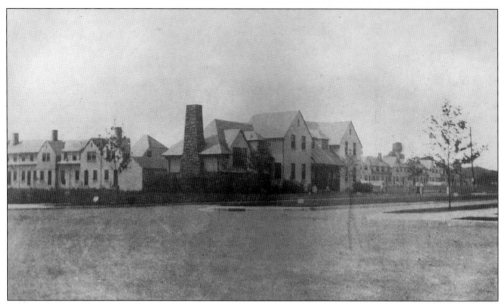

This is the entrance to Overlook Colony, showing the boardinghouse and library (the large center building facing Commonwealth Avenue at the corner of Philadelphia Pike.)

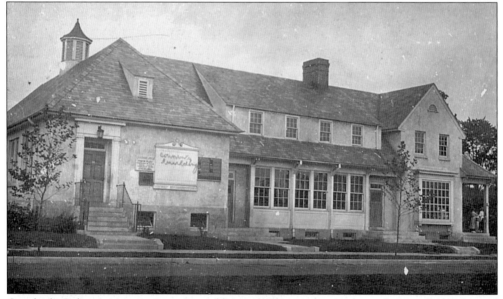

Overlook Colony's community center (General Chemical's employee housing) also housed stores, including Shinn's, and later, Steins. Horse races were held at this location in the late 1800s. Now it is an antique shop and apartments. Also known at one time as Redman's Hall, the Claymont Fire Company started here. The current owners, Dawn Lamb and her parents, received the New Castle County's Preservation Award in 2000. (Courtesy of Dawn Lamb.)

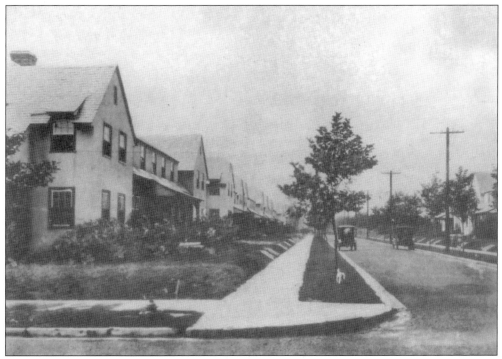

Built between 1911 and 1917, Overlook Colony was employee housing for the General Chemical Company. It was one of three such communities built in this general time period. This scene is of Third Avenue.

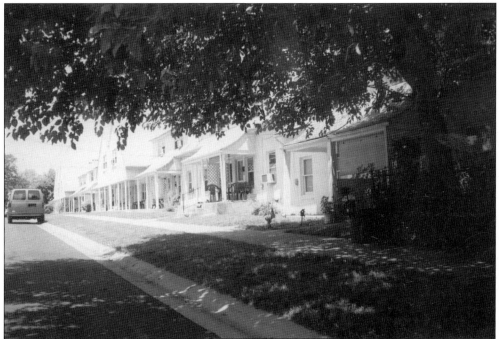

The housing on Second Avenue in Overlook Colony is shown here. Like Worthland, these homes were built by General Chemical as employee housing, but are now privately owned.

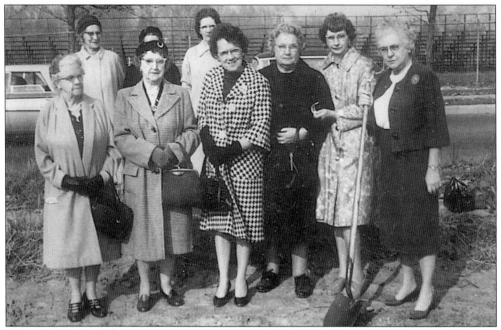

The Woman's Club of Claymont was established in April 1920. Meetings were held in homes, Old Stone School (where they started the Claymont Library), various community buildings, and churches, until they constructed their building in 1965 on Green Street. Pictured here, from left to right, are the following: (first row) Lilly Taylor, Martha Young, Marion Morgan, Louise Haller, Mary Sites, and Miriam Stahl; (second row) Lola Thompson, unidentified, and Wilda Phillips. (Courtesy of Janet Eckman.)

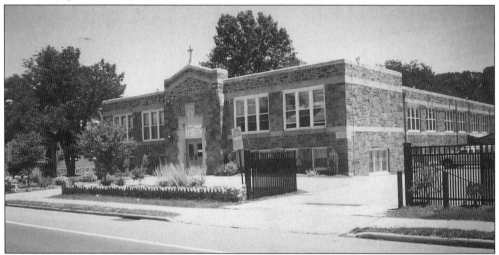

The first Catholic Mass was held in the home of Mr. and Mrs. Joel Gillen in Worthland. The first parish Mass was held January 11, 1920, in the Overlook Colony Community Center, also known as Redman's Hall. In 1921, the Holy Rosary Parish was established at Seminole Avenue and Mass started on September 1. In 1936 the parish's first permanent structure, a school, was built. By 1950, it had eight classrooms and half the building was used for church services. School was taught by Ursiline Sisters. In 1951, the Sisters of St. Joseph came on staff. In 1952, they bought the Worth House for use as a convent for the Sisters of St. Joseph.

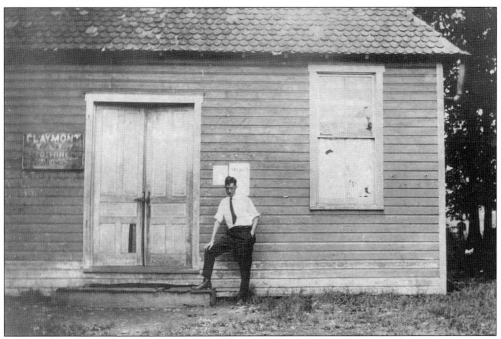

Claymont Community Hall was on Philadelphia Pike, north of the Atonement Methodist Church. This photograph was taken around 1916.

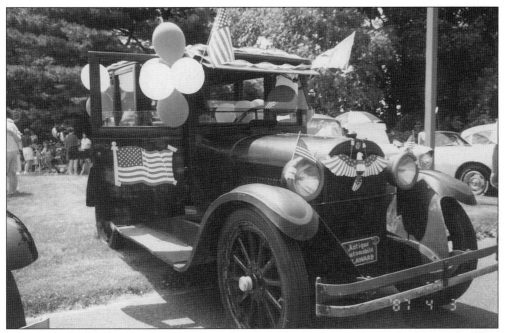

A 1924 Dodge Brothers Business Sedan is decorated for a July Fourth parade. (Courtesy of Jim and Carol Teal, members of the Brandywine Region-Antique Automobile Club of America.)

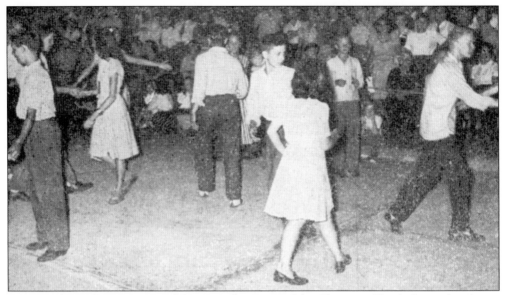

A square dance depicting one of the many functions of the Claymont Youth Council is shown around 1949. The Youth Council was formed primarily to provide summer activities for Claymont-area youth and adults, primarily using school facilities. In 1950, it had over 1,500 individual participants involved in its activities, which included dog obedience, old timer's get-togethers, dramas, dances, concerts, Junior Olympics, and tennis.

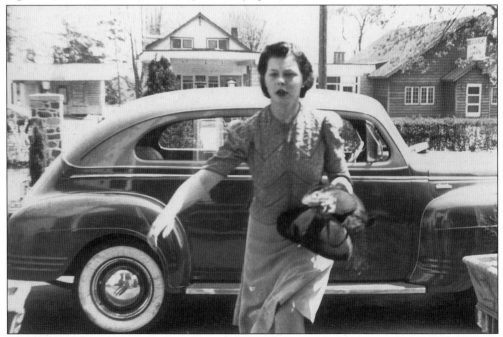

Pictured here is Jean Farrow Robinson, entering the Farrow House. Note that Camp De La Warr is across the street on the east side of Philadelphia Pike. Looking from left to right, the camp buildings shown are a hamburger and soda shop and a restaurant dinning room. There were cabins for rent in the rear. Although significantly remodeled, these buildings still stand. (Courtesy of Daniel Farrow.)

The Claymont Civic League was founded in 1919 by Charles C. Lester Sr., in order to provide leadership for the unincorporated community of Claymont.

CONSTITUTION OF THE COMMUNITY LEAGUE OF CLAYMONT, DELAWARE

ARTICLE I.

The name of the organization shall be "The Community League of Claymont, Delaware."

ARTICLE II.

The objects and purposes for which this League is formed are to improve civic and social conditions in and around Claymont, Delaware; to promote the moral, mental and physical welfare of its members and of the community at large; to generally promote and advance matters pertaining to our public schools; to protect the persons and property of its members and their families from violence and injury; to secure to its members such rights and privileges as are guaranteed to the people under the Constitution of the State of Delaware; and generally, to do all things to further the best interests of the community in any legal and proper manner.

ARTICLE III.

Membership in this League is limited to persons over the age of seventeen years, residing or owning real estate within the boundaries of School District Number One, of Brandywine Hundred, New Castle County, State of Delaware, in addition to such other qualifications as may be defined by the By-Laws of the League.

ARTICLE IV.

Section 1. Its officers shall consist of a President, a First Vice-President, a Second Vice-President, a Secretary, and a Treasurer.

Section 2. Any adult member of the League shall be eligible for the aforesaid offices.

Section 3. The aforesaid officers shall be elected annually, by ballot. Vacancies occurring during the year, shall be filled by the President.

ARTICLE V.

This Constitution may be amended at a stated meeting, of the League by an affirmative two-thirds vote of the members present and voting; provided the proposed amendment has been submitted in writing at the previous stated meeting.

ARTICLE VI.

A quorum for the transaction of business shall consist of forty members present and voting.

SCHEDULE.

Schedule 1. The officers of the League for the first year may be elected at the meeting at which the Constitution is adopted.

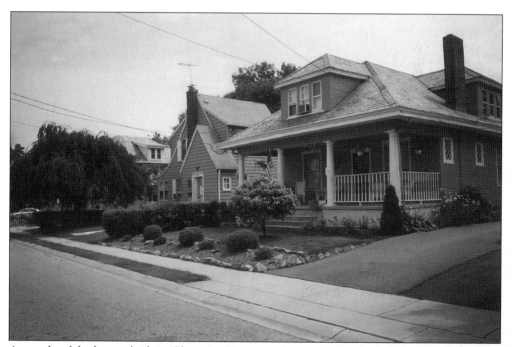

A sample of the homes built in Claymont Terrace, adjacent to Overlook Colony, is shown here around 1925.

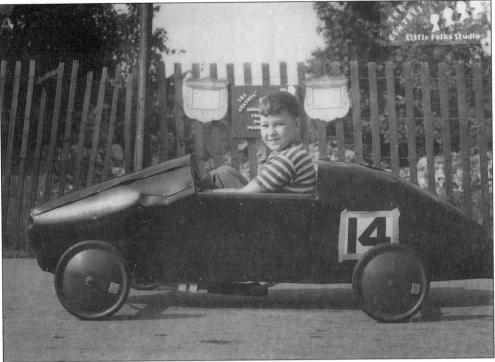

A very young Brice James is shown here in 1948 at the second annual Delaware Association of Police Pushmobile Derby. The derby started in Claymont on Governor Printz Road at Shackley Motors. After two years in Claymont, it moved near Newark, DE, on its own site. The derby is still held annually. (Courtesy of Brice James.)

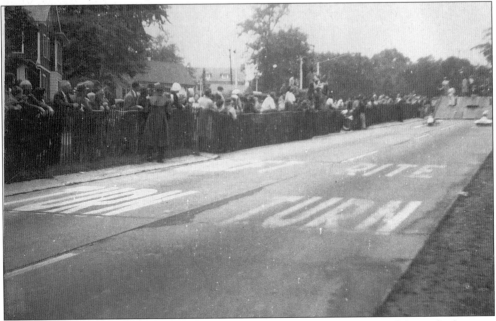

The 1948 Delaware Association of Police Pushmobile Derby is pictured here, looking up Governor Printz Boulevard toward Philadelphia Pike. (Courtesy of Ruth Govatos Stein.)

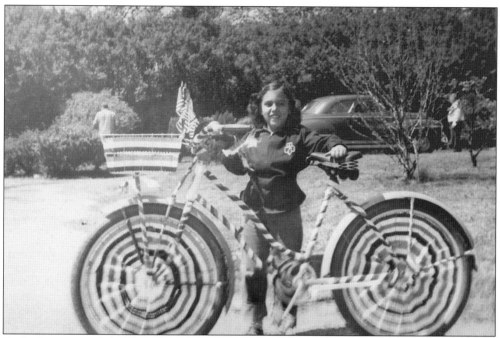

Ruth Govatos with her bicycle decorated for a Memorial Day parade is shown here at "Old Main" on Green Street (Claymont High School). Parades often took place on the Fourth of July and Memorial Day. (Courtesy of Ruth Govatos Stein.)

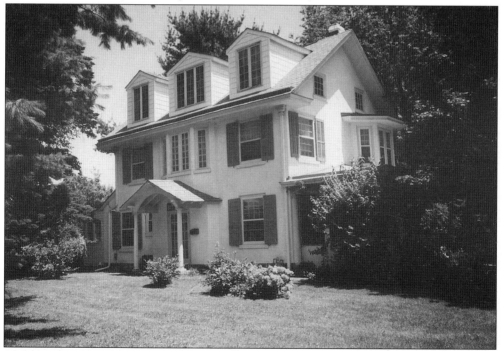

This home on Philadelphia Pike was built by the Worth family for their daughter. Later, it was used as a guest house and today it is a residence. The house is on the south side of the Worth family home, which is now part of the Holy Rosary Church. (Courtesy of Ray Hester.)

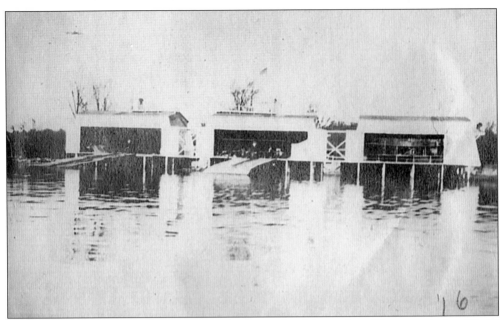

These were the hangers for the seaplane training school located in Claymont during World War I. The buildings stood until the 1940s.

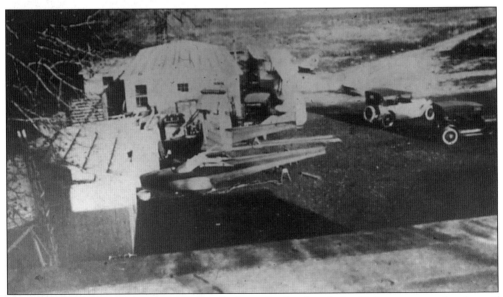

Claymont's Aviation School was located along the banks of the Delaware near the foot of Myrtle Avenue. During World War I it was used to train pilots on sea planes. The hangars stood until about 1940.

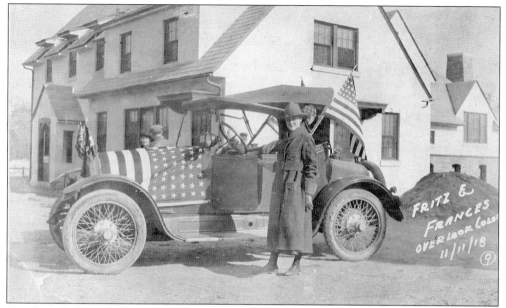

Overlook Colony's boardinghouse and library is the setting of this photograph of a decorated automobile celebrating Armistice Day on November 11, 1918. The war was over and Claymont celebrated. (Courtesy of Dawn Lamb.)

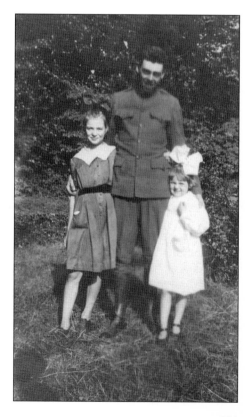

Earl Keen is seen just returning to Claymont from World War I. Shown here, from left to right, are Mildred Hannah, Earl Keen, and Elizabeth Robelen.

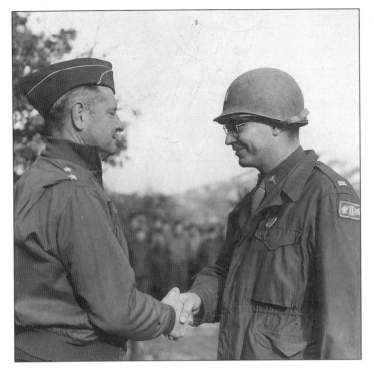

Captain Allen Schiek is pictured here receiving his Bronze Star medal from Gen. Geofrey Keyes. Dr. Schiek received the medal for meritorious service in support of combat operations on the 5th Army Front in North Africa and Italy in 1945. Dr. Schiek practiced dentistry in Claymont from 1938 until 1942, then went into the military. He returned to his wife, Elizabeth, and their daughters in Claymont in 1947, where he practiced dentistry until his death in 1977 at the age of 66.

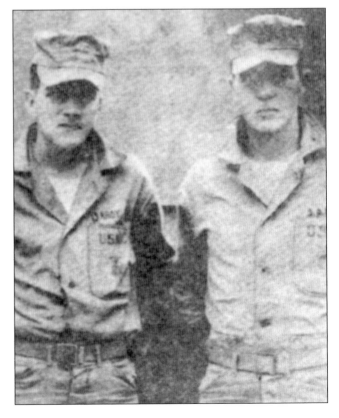

The Brady brothers served in Korean combat with the 1st Marine Division. On the left are Sgt. Joseph J. Brady and Cpl. John P. Brady, sons of Mr. and Mrs. James J. Brady of Forrest Avenue, Claymont. Both graduated from Claymont High School. Joseph went into the service immediately, and John left his job at the A&P store to go. This photograph was taken in August 1953. (Courtesy of David D. Brady.)

David D. Brady of Claymont served proudly in the Korean occupation forces in Japan from 1956 until 1958. His brother Jerry served there in 1954 and 1955. This was typical of Claymont families—almost all of the sons served their country in the military. The Brady boys were sons of James and Celia Brady, immigrants from Scotland and Ireland. (Courtesy of David D. Brady.)

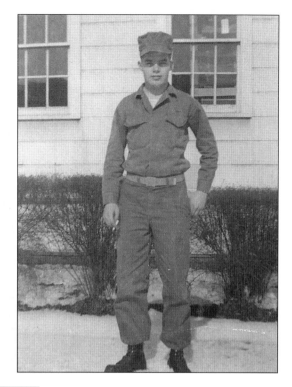

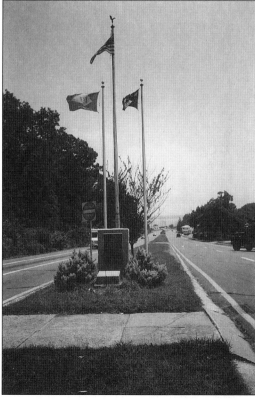

The War Memorials at Governor Printz Road and Philadelphia Pike are in memory of all veterans. The small stone memorial in the front was placed by the Wilmington Chapter No. 1 of the American Gold Star Mothers in memory of their sons, on May 25, 1946. The tall monument was placed by Hall Burke VFW Post 5447 on May 30, 1989, in honor of all veterans. (Courtesy of Ray Hester.)

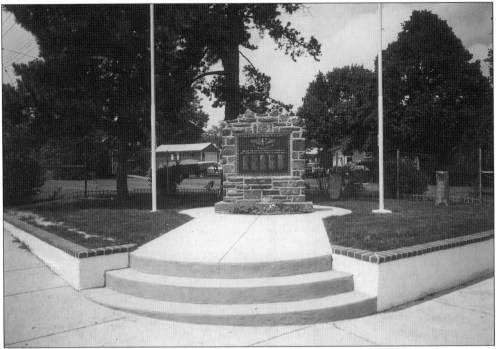

This memorial in Knollwood (Worthland) was placed in honor of the men and women of the Worthland community who served in World War II. Worthland alone, had over 100 men and women who served their country in World War II. (Courtesy of Ray Hester.)

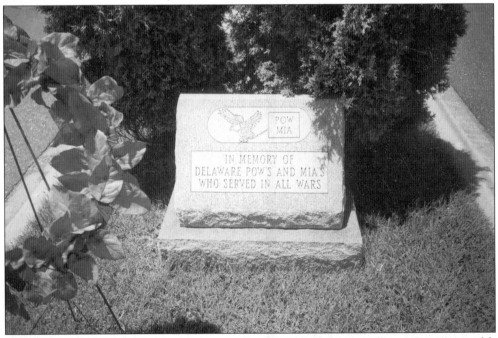

The "Prisoner of War (POW), Missing in Action (MIA) Memorial" on Commonwealth Avenue in Overlook Colony is shown here. Proud of its meaning, the community takes care of this memorial all year long.

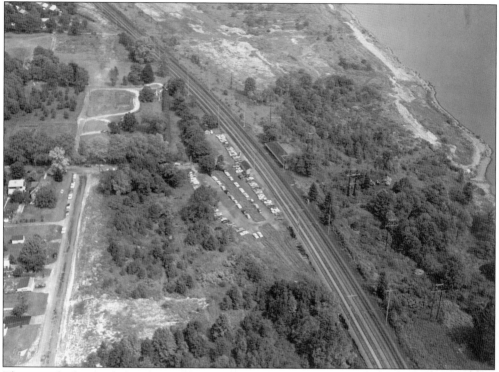

This aerial photo of the eastern part of Claymont shows the east end of Archmere and Claymont Station in the 1950s, prior to I-495 taking a "swath" out along the tracks. (Courtesy of the Delaware Department of Transportation, DELDOT.)

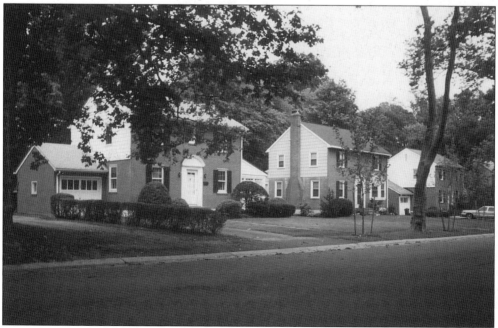

A sample of homes being built in Claymont in the 1940s is shown here. This is Hillside Road, one of Claymont's beautiful, tree-lined streets. (Courtesy of Ray Hester.)

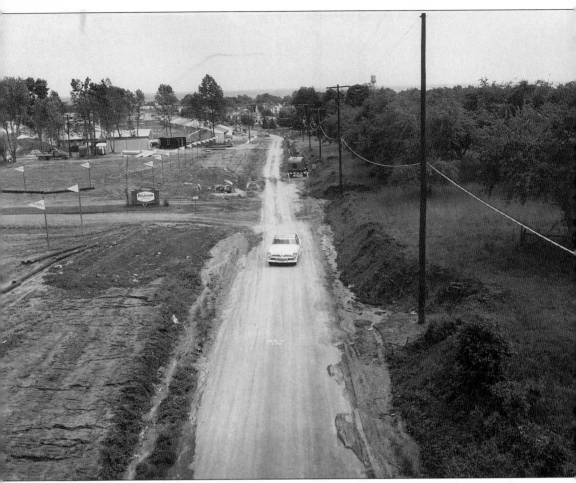

The construction at Radnor Green on Harvey Road is shown here in 1955. The Lesher Farm is on the right. After Mr. Lesher died, this property was sold for development. (Courtesy of the Delaware Department of Transportation, DELDOT.)

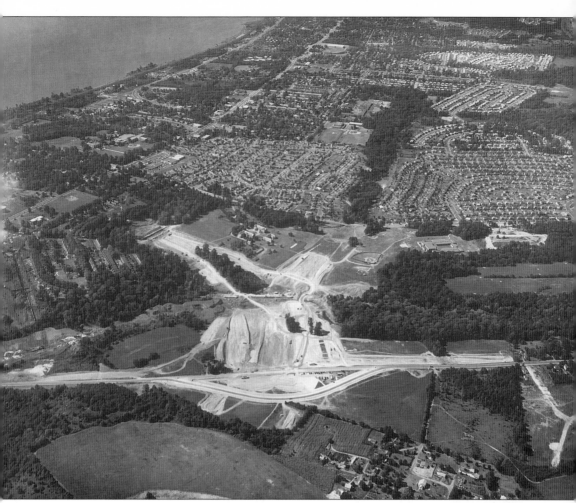

Another aerial view of all of Claymont was taken around 1955. Note the large area of Brookview (center-left) and Ashbourne Hills (center-right). (Courtesy of the Delaware Department of Transportation, DELDOT.)

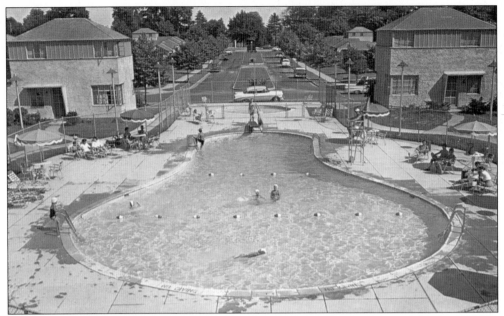

The Brookview Apartments pool along Bayard Drive is shown here in the late 1950s. Brookview was built in 1952 and was considered among the best garden apartments in the area at the time. This photograph looks east towards the Philadelphia Pike. (Courtesy of Allan P. Barrowcliff.)

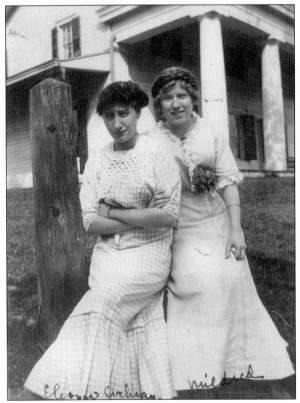

The way we were. Elinor Cochrane and Mildred Casey Lichenstein are shown here at the Robinson House, c. 1918. (Courtesy of Linda K. Rambo.)